# A PLACE CALLED HOME

## THE FCCI STORY

**DR. CARL CONLEY &
DR. REGGIES WENYIKA**

**urban**press

**A Place Called Home**
by Dr. Carl Conley & Dr. Reggies Wenyika
Copyright ©2021 FCCI

ISBN 978-1-63360-167-3

For Worldwide Distribution
Printed in the U.S.A.

Urban Press
P.O. Box 8881
Pittsburgh, PA 15221-0881
412.646.2780
www.urbanpress.us

# Dedication

This book is dedicated to two of FCCI's elders who passed into the presence of the Lord in the past year. Bishop Gaddam Thomas Sr from India and Apostle Augustine Mgala both ended their earthly pilgrimage and are rejoicing in heaven. As we remember them, we are comforted by the words Paul wrote:

*"But we do not want you to be uninformed, brothers and sisters, about those who are asleep, so that you will not grieve as indeed the rest of mankind do, who have no hope. For if we believe that Jesus died and rose from the dead, so also God will bring with Him those who have fallen asleep through Jesus"*
(1 Thessalonians 4:13-14).

The first FCCI meeting was held in a living room. From those humble beginnings, FCCI is now touching leaders in more than 50 nations.

# PREFACE

In July of 2019, I set foot in southern Africa for the first time in almost twenty years. In 2000, I left Zimbabwe and emigrated to the United States with my wife and daughter to pursue further education. With $2000 and two suitcases each, we landed in Tulsa, Oklahoma with a lot of faith and a dream. With no other means of support and having not secured admission into a graduate school or the means to pay for it, it was going to take the hand of God to begin the journey to establish ourselves. Faith, vision, a calling, and trust in God had all motivated me to walk away from a comfortable and secure life for my family. Those early days in the U.S. were difficult. We had been stripped down to nothing but our bare faith, but God was faithful and true to His word.

As I reminisce with joy and thankfulness, I rejoice in what God has done. I graduated from Oral Roberts University with a doctorate and my wife graduated from the University of Oklahoma with her doctorate as well. I am now in my eighth year as a college president in the U.S. Christ and education truly change lives and I have been honored to be an ambassador for both all over the world. However, my story and our story would not be complete without an organization called Faith Community Churches International (FCCI) and Dr. Carl Conley, its founder.

We would not have made it to be where we are today if it wasn't for Dr. Carl and what FCCI represents. This book will tell you how FCCI began, how Dr. Conley and I met, and our work together that has most recently brought me to the place where I have succeeded him as the general superintendent of FCCI. It has been an amazing journey.

However, Dr. Conley is not the only remarkable person I have met through FCCI. In the last section of this book, you will have an opportunity to hear from some of them. You will learn how they got involved in FCCI, for each one of them has their own unique story of what FCCI has meant to them over the years. They will each tell you where they believe FCCI is headed and why, if you are a church leader, you should consider being part of this wonderful missions-minded fellowship. As we tell our stories, we will tell you what FCCI stands for and what we have accomplished along with our dreams and desires for one another and its future.

As mentioned earlier, July of 2019 was the first time I'd been back to southern Africa in almost 20 years and I was there to facilitate and participate in an FCCI International Conference. Our host was Bishop Levy Silindza, the founder and senior minister of Governors Cathedral Church in Boksburg, South Africa. It was a great conference that helped and exposed us to many opportunities that will in all probability take FCCI into a new phase. With the help of Bishop Silindza, plans to reach out to even more leaders and hold meetings with them were made. We had also planned for a follow-up regional conference for the spring of 2020—and then the worldwide COVID-19 pandemic stopped us all in our tracks.

All our plans had to be put on hold, but as I write, we are preparing for our International Conference in Tucson in June 2021 and I am personally excited to see our members and friends again as well as jumpstart our plans for the future. Some of those plans are described in the following pages and others will have to be adjusted to the realities of a post-COVID-19 world—whenever that will be and whatever that looks like.

As you read, you will hear from Dr. Conley and me. Sometimes we will both write a chapter and at other times we wrote alone. In all of it, you will hear our heart for the Church worldwide and our desire to undergird and train leaders by providing relevant materials, educational and inspirational conferences, and meaningful fellowship from which they can learn and be more effective in the work God has called them to do.

We believe the need for what FCCI has to offer has never been greater, and we present this book in the hope that we can reach more with the message that FCCI for all of us is truly what the title of this books says—*A Place Called Home: The FCCI Story.*

Dr. Reggies Wenyika
FCCI General Superintendent
June 2021

Dr. Reggies Wenyika with his wife, Dr. Bongi Wenyika

# INTRODUCTION

In his preface, Dr. Reggies mentioned his trip to Africa in 2019. To be more specific, he was there for our biannual FCCI International Conference that was held in Boksburg, South Africa. Our previous conference in 2017 had been in Blantyre, Malawi, so our intent was to have a conference outside of Africa but the challenge of obtaining a visa for some of our leaders was problematic. Therefore, we decided to return to Africa. Bishop Levy Silindza, one of our FCCI elders, and his church hosted us and did a fabulous job. This conference was unique from all we have had in the past for it was when I turned the reins of FCCI's leadership over to Dr. Reggies.

In 2013, I met with the elders and said, "Brothers and sisters, the years have added up" and I informed them I wanted to step down (more on that later). I've never really desired to be the head of anything, I just want to serve, and that is why I consented in the first place to lead FCCI. If our members felt I could help them, then I wanted and was willing to do so. In 2013, they urged me to continue to serve and I agreed, but by 2019 a few health challenges told me it was the right time to make the transition.

I also knew it was time because FCCI could benefit from certain giftings I don't have. To be honest, my gifting is on a small, short list. My most significant gift is that I love people and want to encourage them to be what they can become. I knew I couldn't take the organization where it needed to go. I've realized that for the last six or seven years. What I've already seen in just a few months since our transition has encouraged my heart, even though COVID-19 has affected all we have tried to do. If God will help me, I want to use the energy and time I have remaining to develop FCCI's presence in the U.S. Because I had to give so much of my time internationally during my time as president, I feel like the U.S. has not developed as we had hoped.

Our leaders and leadership team felt like the Lord had prepared the way for my stepping down (but not going away). Dr Reggies is honored and respected wherever he goes, and whenever and wherever he ministers, people love him as much as and perhaps more than me. I think sometimes they put up with me, but they love him. I was looking forward to this transition because I knew it was God's timing, His ordained event. I thought the setting in Johannesburg was quite appropriate for we were doing it in Africa where we have many pastors and churches—and it is Dr. Reggies' home continent.

Somebody said it's rare to see leadership turned over to an African. I never, ever think in terms of someone being an African or Indian or whatever. I was raised with the Papago Native Americans and I learned only to think people. I never thought of it in terms of turning the leadership over to an African man. I thought of it as turning it over to God's man. Therefore, it was a privilege to set in Dr. Reggies as general superintendent both legally and publicly while in the presence of our brethren and as president of Faith Community Churches International. It just was a great honor for me. It was a joy to see it happen and also witness how the brethren responded to him—and how they continue to respond to him.

In the past, we had most of our conferences set up like an auditorium but in Johannesburg we had a classroom setting in the church sanctuary. They moved out the chairs and set up tables, so it was easier to take notes. Everything was beautifully and efficiently done. Also in the past, we had our meals served in a different venue like when we met in Roanoke, Virginia and Malawi. This time, we had our meals served right where we held our general sessions, and it made a world of difference.

One of the highlights, apart from the succession cere-mony, was our ordination service. We had our elders from vari-ous regions and nations present candidates who were called and qualified for ministry, and we laid our hands on them to recognize and set them apart for God's purpose and work. As we look to the future of FCCI with the leadership succession, it blessed and excited me to see so many young people and even senior people who felt called of God to go into ministry. When I saw them answer the call and put themselves out there, saying "I'm giving my life to this," I was inspired.

From a personal standpoint, I have been part of two church organizations, and both didn't work out so well. I'm not against organizations, but I've seen many people hurt by organizations that started out as a fellowship and ended up legalistic and controlling. Consequently, I've seen young ministers fear being a part of something beyond their local work because they saw it not go well for their father, mother, or other relative. That is the reason I wanted FCCI to be a fellowship and I pray it never becomes anything else. I wanted something that would serve people and not control them, an entity that would give and not look for what it could get.

My contribution to this book will be the history of FCCI which ties in with my own history, so you will read about my experiences that helped shape FCCI. I will also tell you more about my relationship with Dr. Reggies and why I know he is the right man for the job of general superintendent in the years ahead. All this has been a pleasant experience for me, for it has given me a chance to reminisce about the wonderful memories I have of FCCI. And to think that this book will contribute to its future is a happy thought as well, so without further delay, let's get into *A Place Called Home: The FCCI Story.*

Dr. Carl Conley
Tucson, Arizona
June 2021

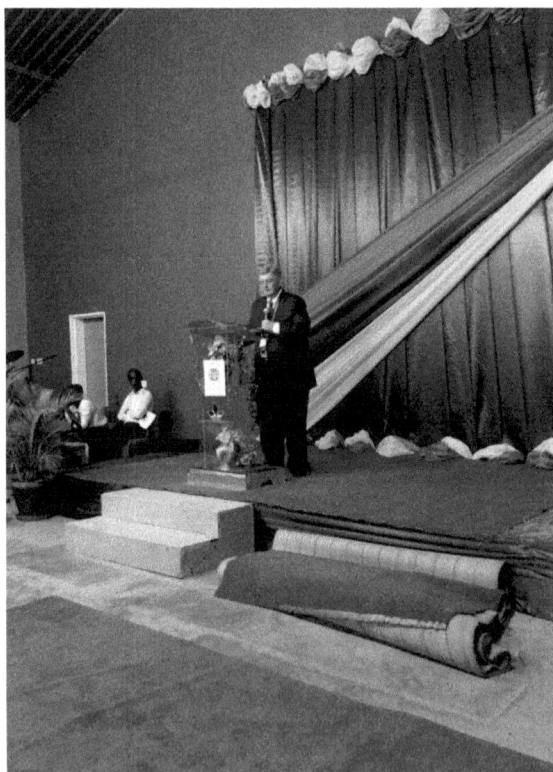

Dr. Carl speaks at the biannual conference in Malawi in 2017.

# CHAPTER ONE

# How FCCI Started

*Dr. Carl*

Let me start by telling some of my personal story which will explain why I have such a heart for missions and working among people who don't look or think like me. As I mentioned, I was raised among the Pagago Native Americans. Papago was a name somebody assigned them a long time ago, but they have since reverted to their name in their native language which is *Tohono O'odham*. It means *desert people*. My mother had a vision when she was 16 years old that she would be working among people with a very dark skin color. She knew they were not of African descent, but in those days, all she had to consult was an encyclopedia, so she never found a picture of what she had seen in her vision.

She became quite ill when my brother and I were young, and the doctor told my father to bring her out West in order for her to live longer. She had contracted tuberculosis and had hardening of the arteries. After we moved to the West, one day Dad took us for a ride. We headed to Sells, Arizona where there is a Papago reservation. We were driving through a little village when my mother started crying hysterically. As a young boy, I was scared and thought she was dying: "What's the matter, Mama? What's the matter?"

"These are the people, "she responded. "These are the people I saw in my vision!" Sure enough, they were not Negroid but were very dark. I could share so much more but in short, God

1

healed my mother of all her ailments and she went on to start five churches among the Papago people. Dad was supportive of Mom's work, but he was a construction superintendent in Tucson, Arizona and not involved in the ministry.

I grew up speaking their language and thinking I was a Native American. I loved those people and living there imparted to me a tribal worldview. Many years later, I came to realize how God had prepared me when I was in India and people asked me, "How is it that you understand us when missionaries who have been here 40 years don't understand us at all?" I prayed about it and the Lord showed me that I have a tribal worldview.

It made sense to me. I grew up in a tribe. That's the way I was raised. Whoever's house I was in when it was time to eat, I ate. If I ended up some place at night and it was time to sleep, I slept. Wherever I was, I was one of those kids and I grew up that way. It was so second nature that I never realized my worldview is quite different from the one most Americans possess.

Growing up, of course I attended church but never had an official role. After I got married and moved away, I came back to the West to pastor among the Apaches in New Mexico. We built a church there along with an educational center and a parsonage. Then we moved to Albuquerque in 1967 and I assumed the oversight of a little church with about 20 people. We had a small building and when the rain came, it flooded us out. I took that church as a mission and God helped us.

The Lord showed me property that was across the street from a school for Native American children, and those schools were prevalent back in those days. I had other workers from my denomination tell me that I was not wise to try and build there. But I knew if I wanted to reach Native Americans, what better place to do it than the place they all had to come—their school.

I went to see the man who owned it and said, "I want to buy your property."

He replied, "It's not for sale."

"But the Lord has already told me I'm going to build a church on your property. You've got to sell it to me." I went to see him every week.

Finally, he said. "I guess I'm going to have to sell this to you. Otherwise, you're going to drive me crazy."

I said, "You're right."

Anyway, we built an adobe church there even though we had no means to do so. I preached for six weeks before we moved in on the subject of giving. After the first message, we received the largest offering we'd ever had in any month. We never ever had a financial need.

All the tribal people were very kind to me. I did not see myself as different than they were and I hope that came across to them. I was one of them who happened to be called to pastor and I related to them as I would anyone else. I know God prepared me for that through my upbringing. They were people I loved. The Lord sent me there to be with them and they were kind enough to receive me. Once I arrived, I gave them all the energy and love I had. That is a pretty simple formula I have followed wherever I go.

A few years ago, I was in Nigeria when someone asked me, "How does it feel being around so many foreigners?" I thought, "Are you kidding me? I'm very honored they let me be here." I didn't feel different or superior when I was there or anywhere God has taken me to minister. I'm actually always blown away that they want to hear anything I've got to say.

When I first began to pastor, I did not have seminary training but then I attended an Assembly of God Bible college and continued until I earned a master's in theology. After Albuquerque, Ellene and I moved to Phoenix where I worked for years with two different organizations. W. T. Jeffers, who used to be the editor for Oral Roberts University's material, started an organization called Feed My Children and then changed it to World Changers.

While I was pastoring the church in Albuquerque, he approached me for help because they wanted to sponsor Native American children, so I helped them identify about 2,000 children to help. I traveled to two states for that project and then they wanted me to be the national director, but I said, "No, I'm a pastor. I'm not a traveling person." Then they asked if I was willing to help them occasionally. That grew into where I was working full-time for them *and* pastoring the church.

At that point, I went to the church and informed them I was going to resign. I had been training a few of the local men to be leaders and informed them that they needed to take over the church. When I had first met them, they were living in poverty but after a while, they had faithfully applied godly principles to their lives and were thriving. I assigned them duties and I stayed involved for about a year. Then finally, I turned it over to them while I went full time with World Changers, and went on to open offices in nine different countries. Later, I was missions director of the Don Stewart Association, and finally brought him into the Assemblies of God at one point. Don was the successor to A. A. Allen, the famous faith healer and evangelist. I was with his group on two different occasions and ran his missions and crusades department.

Then I went back to Santa Fe, New Mexico, and started a church. After I was there for a while, I came to Tucson to pastor the First Assembly of God. After that, I returned to the Don Stewart Association for a season until we had a difference of opinion over some ministry philosophy matters. When the Association started to raise money through direct mail, I was not comfortable with some of their approaches to that.

When I left, we started two organizations in Albuquerque by the name LifeLink. LifeLink was a humanitarian relief organization that was under LifeLink International, which was the church. FCCI, which is the focus of this book, was then started as the international division of LifeLink International in 1987.

Eventually, I left Albuquerque to join Buddy Harrison in Tulsa. I was with his organization for 16 years including four years after he passed away. Buddy Harrison and I were quite close. We *never* had a cross word with one another. It was like we were raised in the same house. We thought alike, the only difference being that he was a lot smarter than I. He was a very dear brother.

When we started LifeNet humanitarian work, we had many shelters for children and those in need. I was trying to find support for that work, and we started to feel the need to shift our emphasis overseas because of some of the needs we were discovering. At the time, I talked to one of my board members who was a good friend of Buddy Harrison's. I said to my friend, "I need to find some substantial support for our work." He offered to help me target independent churches to meet with and ask for help, but I knew that would take too long.

Then he said, "I've got a good friend in Tulsa. They are having their conference two weeks from now. Why don't I mention it to him and let's see if you can make contact? He has a fellowship of churches. Maybe they would get behind you." To make a long story short, he made the connection with Buddy Harrison who invited me to come. I got there on Sunday night. He held his first conference session on Monday morning, and I got there just as his session was finishing. He came out, we met, and he asked me to speak to his pastor the next morning at breakfast. The name of Buddy's organization was Faith Christian Fellowship (FCF).

From then on, we connected—there is no other way to describe it. He said, "Would you go to India for me? We have a work that's in trouble. We don't know exactly what's going on, but something's wrong." I made that trip for him and was there for seven weeks, resolving some problems and getting many things ironed out.

And then Buddy asked, "Would you please come in and run our missions department?" I helped him structure that and finally I moved to Tulsa from Santa Fe to do what I could for the organization. As I said, I was there for 16 years but when Buddy died and his wife took over the organization, I eventually returned to Tucson four years later. I came back to be with Pastor Louise Brock, who had been one of the leaders from almost the beginning of FCF with Buddy Harrison. Her son, Bruce, had been our area director. He still pastors a church in Tucson. Both Louise and Bruce urged me to come to Tucson and I have been there since 2003.

I love Tucson. I was raised close by, so it was good to return. We debated between going back to Albuquerque or Tucson, but we felt we did what the Lord wanted us to do. I don't know exactly how FCF is doing now. Pat's gifts were quite different than Buddy's, and I understand that Pat has now retired from the presidency and has turned it over to her daughter. I wish them the best. I have no bad feelings toward them or their work, and don't regret my time there. I learned a great deal during my time there.

The roots of FCCI go deeper than FCF, back to before I ever met or worked with Buddy Harrison. FCCI goes back to LifeLink and LifeLink International when we were in Santa Fe. We had those two corporations going before I ever met Buddy Harrison and FCCI was a subsidiary of LifeLink International. Therefore, our corporate name is LifeLink International and FCCI is a division of LifeLink International. It's a New Mexico corporation. LifeLink is the humanitarian branch but I am no longer the president. I resigned from that, but they insisted I stay on the board.

We came to Tucson feeling we were obeying the Lord. Bruce Brock had promised to support our work with $1,000 a month. That was the sum total of our income. I bought the house we are still in with a $1,000 payment and today it's paid for. I've traveled the world for the last twenty years and the Lord has always provided. We have never been beggars. We simply trusted the Lord and started serving.

When I left FCF, it was rather abrupt as transitions sometimes go in ministry. The leadership felt a change needed to be made, but when my friends heard about my transition, their emails flooded my inbox because I had built many close relationships with people all over the world. I had been reestablished as FCF vice president in June, but I resigned the second week of July after our annual conference. People called me from Nigeria and from all over the world to say I couldn't quit. "We need you. We look to you for help and support. You're still our father." This was all due in part to a policy FCF had that nobody from the field could contact anybody in the office. If anybody did call or write, they referred them to me: "Carl will be back next Tuesday. Call back then." So I was the only one in that international organization who ever had any contact with any of the international members of FCF.

In the minds of many of our international friends, I was and had been FCF to them. Many I had known over the years, even in the States, came into FCF because of me. That helped their work grow. Many of those same people left FCF, not because of my departure, but because the organization had changed their rules and regulations for the members who were in the missions field. I never advised anybody to leave FCF. Yet they kept saying, "We still need to be associated with you." I had no income or way for them to do that. I realized, however, that the Lord had not relieved me of my responsibility to care for them and I knew God had to help me find a way to fulfill that duty—which He did. I continued to serve and the Lord continued to make it possible.

At first, I began to operate under LifeLink International. Bruce Brock, who was one of the main pastors and supporters of what I was doing, said he didn't like that name. The name of his church was Faith Community Church, so I suggested, "How does Faith Community Church International (FCCI) sound?" and he liked the sound of it. That's how we adopted that name—FCCI, a division of LifeLink International.

When we returned to Tucson from Tulsa, I continued to support those international friends who had been part of FCF in practical and spiritual matters. I started visiting and teaching them as the Lord would provide. Pastor Bruce asked me once, "Carl, what do you do when you go over there? When I get invited, I go but what am I going to tell them? I think they know more than I do."

I responded, "Pastor Bruce, what I do is help them with whatever they ask me to do. If they need help with administration. I have tried to do that. If they want help with training leaders, I try to do that. Whatever I've got to give them, I give. If they ask me for it, I'll give it to them." I continued, "Some people have told me I'm a gate kicker. I get there and I find I'm standing at the gate and they don't know what to do, so I kick the gate open and get out of the way." That's what I did. I responded to the call from the field. I tried to do whatever they asked me to do.

When we started FCCI, Pastor Bruce had been having a quarterly regional conference as part of FCF, in addition to the annual FCF conference. Then when FCCI started, Bruce, his mother, Louise, and I were the three original elders. Bruce eventually stepped out of any eldership role, but he's still loosely connected to the fellowship. In those early days, we had our first FCCI conference at his church. Initially, we had one every year, but then decided having one every other year was a bit easier on those who had to travel from long distances and foreign countries.

The structure for our conferences was actually designed by Felix Omobude from Nigeria, who you will hear more about later. He suggested we should not ask the local church to support these meetings after we had the first one but instead, he suggested we should financially undergird the next one ourselves. He recommended we receive faith promises and use that money from those promise to fund the next conference. Felix is effective at raising funds, so he raised our first budget at our first meeting for the second meeting and that's how we have operated ever since. The first international event we held was in Malawi in 2017; prior to that, they had all been in the States.

The one we held in Malawi was a great success as was the one in South Africa that Dr. Reggies mentioned earlier. Malawi was five times bigger in terms of attendance then we had in South Africa. We would have had a lot more people in South Africa if those interested could have gotten travel visas. The one in Malawi went $10,000 over budget, but I had seen it coming so I had prepared accordingly.

I first met Dr. Reggies through FCF when he was a doctoral student at ORU. At first, Dr. Reggies was my gopher. If I needed anything, I called on Reggies and he was always there for me. When we had our conference in Roanoke, Virginia, he asked, "What can I do to help?" I said, "Get there three days early to welcome people because I have to speak here on Sunday. I can't be there until Monday morning." So he went three days early to greet the people as they came in. Everything I've ever needed, he's the guy I called. He's always been there for me. If I had ever had a son, I would have wanted him to be Reggies.

★★★★★

*Dr. Reggies*

Shortly after I came to the States, I was ordained through a church in Pennsylvania. When an ongoing relationship with that church didn't work out, I came back to Tulsa and had no one with whom to fellowship. I was homeless and had nowhere to go as far as church was concerned. The man I was working for at Oral Roberts University named David Dorries was ordained through FCF. He told me about the organization, but I had already heard of it because an African missionary named Jeff Rogers from Zimbabwe was in town at that time preaching at an FCF church.

I knew Jeff well so I asked him for more information about FCF. He offered to introduce me to their director of missions who was Carl Conley. When he introduced us, Carl said, "Hey, let's meet soon. If you have anything you need, let me know." Many people say that and don't mean it, but Carl meant it. I followed him to his office and that is the end, or should I say the beginning of the story. I had found a home.

The Lord truly provided and worked quickly to bring it all together. I was a spiritual orphan looking for a father and a place to land. I became part of FCF but found it difficult to do more and expand my role there beyond just being a member or volunteer. As the FCF conference in 2002 got under way in Roanoke, it was my job to greet people. I picked up most of the brothers from other countries at the airport who were in FCF and that's how I got to meet and know them, including Felix Omobude from Nigeria.

During the conference, I noticed how no one paid much attention to our international guests, so I started entertaining them, taking them to lunch and things like that. Then Carl held a meeting for the African brothers in his suite so he could make sure he connected with all of them during the busy and full conference days. He was always eating with them or finding other ways to fellowship. That's when I heard some of them question how relevant FCF was for them at that point while expressing their need for something different. For the most part, I learned Felix and others came to those conferences to be with Carl.

I heard someone ask, "What happens if Carl is not here anymore? Where do we fit in to FCF? We need to fellowship more intentionally amongst ourselves so we can get to know each other. Then we need to make a decision as to what happens to our future." Not long after that conference, we all received an email that FCF had eliminated the missions department and therefore Carl was no longer associated with the ministry. All those who had met Carl in his suite then bombarded Carl with requests to do something different just for them.

That's when Carl decided we were going to form FCCI. Carl urged all of us not to leave our organizations: "That's not my heart. I'm not trying to hurt FCF. Please stay where you are." We still tell people to this day, "Stay a part of where you are even if you want to be part of FCCI. "

Sure enough, the following year when Pastor Bruce sponsored a meeting in Tucson, all the African brothers who had gathered in the hotel in Tulsa were there and we've continued our relationship from that point. All our conferences and meetings were in the States until Malawi in 2017 and South Africa in 2019. We went there because we found it difficult to meet our budget having our conference in the States. What's more, the people who wanted to come to the conference were local pastors from all over the world and they often could not obtain visas to travel or raise the money to come to the U.S.

★★★★★

*Dr. Carl*

Now that Dr. Reggies is assuming FCCI's leadership, I'm seeing the future more clearly. It's the vision we had in the beginning that the Lord wants His people to be and work together, not to have an elite or standoff-ish mentality. I've never exhibited that attitude. I was part of the Assemblies of God for years, but I was viewed by some to be a bit of a rebel because I was willing to work with anybody and usually I found the "anybodys" wanted to work with me. I've always had that spirit of cooperation and acceptance. I've never had a sectarian spirit and I don't see one bit of that in Reggies.

The Lord wanted us to provide a spiritual home to a lot of people who needed a home. They needed a place where people would accept and love them but still challenge them to be all they can become. That's been the emphasis throughout my ministry career: Love the people where they are but challenge them to go farther and become what they can be. At the same time, I have never raised money from members for any administrative needs. We have let everyone know when someone had a need, and we have taken pledges for the biannual conference budget but we did not raise money for offices or my support.

We also don't recruit. We simply accept those who feel like we can be useful. Most come in because they have been recommended by someone or through relationships with FCCI members. If I had accepted everybody who wanted to be a part of FCCI, we'd have 20,000 members by now. Unless I know someone, however, or know who is recommending them, I don't accept them. Until I can go where they minister to meet them, their family, and their work, I would not approve their participation. There are some leaders out there who are joining organizations, but often for the wrong reasons.

Our conferences have been referred to as family events because they feel very much like a family reunion. When we come together, the speakers at our events are people we know. When we first started, it was because we felt people needed a home and a place to belong. They didn't need to come and listen to a big-name minister speak to them, who would also require a large speaking fee. We came together and spoke to each other, sharing with one other what the Lord was saying to us. We enjoyed fellowship and ate together, meaning all the leaders, speakers, and attendees ate in the same room. I did not want to communicate that there was a hierarchy or that the leaders were deserving of special treatment. Also, we've never sent invitations to or publicized our events. Maybe the time is coming when we will do that but that will be up to Dr. Reggies and the elders to decide.

★★★★★

### Dr. Reggies

That's been our style. People quickly perceive there are no barriers between one group or another. We have no expectations that the leaders will be served. We want everyone to know the leaders and speakers are all the same and on the same team. No one prevents anyone from talking, eating, or spending time with anyone else.

★★★★★

## Dr. Carl

When I was with FCF, it would surprise people when they called to make an appointment to see me and I would readily agree. They were trying to see other leaders but could not ever get a time to meet. That person would usually say, "Call Carl Conley at FCF. He'll talk to you." A number of the FCF ministers now in the field are in their place because they came to my office and I talked to them. I'd listen to them and help them strategize how to structure their ministry. I never could figure out why any organization would not take the time to listen to the people they purported to be training and serving.

★★★★★

## Dr. Reggies

We intentionally make sure there are no barriers. For example, there's no registration fee to come to the conference. We pool money together from our members to make it possible for anybody to come. We trust that people who benefit from this will stretch out their hand and extend their heart to say, "I want to support you in what you're doing."

At the same time, as Carl mentioned, we don't recruit members. In fact, we get requests regularly asking, "How do I join?" We respond: "We don't know who you are. Let's get to know one another first." If someone doesn't want to do that, then it raises a red flag for us. We then refer them to someone who is part of the FCCI family in their country or region who can follow up and get to know them. Then we are glad to welcome them once one of our family members have met with them and can endorse their ministry. Obviously, some people believe that since our organization was founded in U.S., we can give them financial support. That is not how it works with us.

We are a network of leaders. Our primary focus is on the personal and professional development of those leaders who in turn do the outreach. Those leaders are doing wonderful work. They have a bigger following than we have. They don't need someone from a home office telling them how to do certain things they already know how to do—or requesting they send their already thin resources to maintain a headquarters.

If and when we visit them in the field, we want to empower them to do a better job at what they do within their context. It's not one size fits all. We don't have rules that we impose everywhere we go. We adapt to the local rules and cultural climate as we go. We want people to say, "I feel like they really helped me and I'm not broke after they leave. I'm not having to receive special offerings for the next two years to pay off their conference or visits." We want to empower one another in a way that leads to tangible results.

When we held our conference in Malawi, I followed up with Augustine, our local elder, to ask, "Exactly how has your ministry been different since we were there? Give me tangible results." For example, there was almost a church split among some of those who came to our Malawi event, but because they came and participated, the leaders felt empowered to lead and everybody became more supportive of one another and is on board.

Our conference also enhanced our member's position and stature in the region and their country. After we left, the government recognized the local leaders who were able to host an international conference in their country. And that's why a lot of leaders find it good and easy to associate with us. There's no burden of membership. We trust that people will be responsible enough to want to support our work. That's the FCCI story and it has created a place called home for many of us.

★★★★★

### Dr. Carl

Not everybody who wants to be a part has proven to be responsible over time. There are some people who will take everything you will give them and give nothing back in return. However, some have become valued and faithful partners and it has been a joy and blessing to work with them. People asked me, "How long will you personally keep on doing what you're doing?" My response is, "As long as God's call is there and the people still want me—and the Lord provides." If any of those are not happening, then I'm relieved of my responsibility.

When I first started, I had often prayed, "Lord, You've called me to this work. I'm going to do the best I can to do it, but I'm never going to become a beggar doing it." In my early days of ministry, people labeled and called me an Assembly of God missionary to the Indians. I hated the term. I was a pastor. I was never a missionary. I said, "I'm going to go into business and be independently wealthy. I don't want to ask anybody for *anything*. I'll do God's ministry and pay for it, thank you very much. I don't want anyone's money." That was my attitude, but it was a wrong attitude. To try to earn the money we needed, I went into real estate and owned 30 or so apartments in downtown Phoenix. One year, when the unemployment rate increased to 14%, my business went every way but under. I was literally hours away from filing for bankruptcy.

I had some equity in my house, a little bit of equity in the car I owned, and $3,000 in the bank. I was walking down the street after I dropped my car off to be serviced on a hot July day in Phoenix when I threw my hands in the air and cried out, "Okay, Lord. Do you want the church? You want the business? You want the car? You want the house? You want the wife? You want the child? Okay, You've got it all. I give them all to you to do with as You please, not as I want. I will follow your way with no questions asked." I came to realize the Lord never wanted me to be independent in *anything* I did. He wanted me to be totally dependent on Him and would use others to provide my needs. So that's where I've been ever since and the Lord has faithfully provided every need.

The FCCI leadership structure emerged from my experience as a pastor. We had a corporate board of directors to fulfill our legal requirements to have governing oversight of the finances and the organization's purpose or mission. When I had a church board, I made it clear I would never have a member on the board unless they were first an elder. (I defined an elder as somebody who was mature, demonstrated spiritual maturity, and who had served the church well.)

When we started FCCI, there were just four or five of us who were linked together strongly enough and knew one another well enough to consider ourselves a board of directors and eldership for the organization. First, there was Louise, Bruce, and I—the three founding elders and directors. Our feeling was that the spiritual leadership of the organization should be senior people who exhibited proven apostolic ministry in the sphere where they lived.

As time went on and FCCI grew, men like Felix Omobude from Nigeria, who I had been close to for a number of years, came into FCCI. When I was part of FCF, I had visited his ministry sometimes twice a year. After he joined, we asked him to become part of the eldership and, then one by one, we asked other people to join, men like the late Bishop G. Thomas of India, a man who had more than 200 churches in India. (Bishop G.'s son has now assumed the leadership of that ministry after his father's death in February 2021.) Felix was the one who suggested that we should appoint Bishop Thomas as an elder. The ones we brought in as elders were those who were recommended to me or leaders I knew who had something in them that could benefit the organization's members.

One by one, people have been added as we felt the Lord direct us. For example, when we were in South Africa, Reggies came to me and said, "I feel like we should bring in Bishop Levy Silindza as an elder." Since Reggies is the general superintendent, he didn't need my approval to do it but he discussed it with all the elders—and they agreed. That's the way we've always conducted our business. I didn't appoint somebody as an elder without discussing it with the other elders. If that was something I was feeling in my heart and that person could add something to us and the elders agreed, they would be added.

Speaking of important people who served FCCI, there is one person who has always been there with me to support and strengthen me in the work we had been called to. That person is my wife Ellene, so I asked her to write something from her perspective about our journey. Let's hear from her in the next chapter.

# CHAPTER TWO

# A Family Involved

*Ellene Conley*

Carl and I met in Tucson at First Assembly of God Church, part of the denomination in which I had been raised. I was the pianist there so the pastor called one day to say, "The man we are having here is going to be singing and we need you to play for him." At the time, I was also a student at the University of Arizona where I was majoring in home economics education. When we met, Carl was just out of Bible school. I didn't think I would marry Carl or anyone at that time in my life since marriage wasn't really on my mind.

When I graduated, I taught for a while and as Carl and I prepared for marriage, it became evident he was going to be a pastor. I'm not a speaker, but my area of contribution to any ministry in which we have been involved was music along with organization and administration—and some teaching. I was always quite involved in our churches; I just didn't have a public role.

After we got married in Tucson, the first place we went was Panama City, Florida to serve in the First Assembly Church there, which was the second largest Assembly of God church in the world at that time with maybe 1,500 people. Carl served as the assistant pastor and had oversight for 150 teachers and leaders in Sunday School. We did a daily radio broadcast and a weekly telecast, both of which were quite progressive in 1959. Today, they are commonplace.

From there, we went into Native American work, first in Mescalero, New Mexico and then in Albuquerque. We were there for five years. We finished building a church, then built an educational facility, and finally a parsonage. In Mescalero, we worked with people of the Apache tribe which was such interesting work. They are intense people, but when they met and served the Lord, they loved just as intensely as they expressed their anger when settling their differences.

There was no middle ground with the Apaches. They either loved you or they didn't. We had the most wonderful experience there and we loved it—and them. Our only daughter was born while we were there. Then we went to Albuquerque and we had another wonderful experience. There really wasn't much there until after we built the new church. Everybody helped building it and we had people from 18 different tribes in attendance.

When I say everybody worked, I mean *everybody*. The women dug the foundation and they told anyone who would listen that they were involved—they were proud of their accomplishment for the Lord and the church. It was fascinating to see those 18 tribes come together to work as one, which only the Spirit of the Lord could accomplish. Let me give you an example of their differences, which exist among all people groups when they come together to worship the Lord.

Those of the Navajo tribe loved mutton and would cook it outside. We had a church picnic where they were cooking but we were just having hot dogs, hamburgers, and things like that. There was a lady there from the Acoma tribe, who came to me when there was smoke all around me as I stood close to where they were cooking. This lady came to warn me saying, "Sister, move away from there. You're going to smell like a Navajo!" We just smiled and enjoyed all the small cultural differences like that which made each group different, but then watched as the Holy Spirit knit them into one church body.

While I never worked with Native Americans before our church work, I never had any problem getting along with anyone. They are wonderful people. They are not always demonstrative people who are quick to show outward affection, but when we got to know their heart, we found they were generous and kind.

Our church was right across the street from the Native American school where their children attended at the time. Those were boarding schools where the Native children would live for nine months during the school year. Then in the summer, we would visit each of their homes and once again witness all the different customs of the various tribes.

Carl promised them that if they attended church 90% of the Sundays during the school year, he would visit them in the summer. He did that to encourage attendance and we ended up going to a lot of different places every summer. That meant sometimes we would have to go to Colorado to find one of the students who lived with their family at 10,000 feet above sea level! We loved it. My daughter and I went too. I was a part of everything, although we didn't do much singing—but I organized the trips.

Then things with Carl's ministry began to shift and change. W. T. Jeffers was the first person who came to the conclusion that Carl had something to offer internationally. Prior to that, we were Assembly of God people who served behind the scenes in local church settings, but W. T. saw value in my husband. He encouraged him and gave him responsibility and an opportunity to build on it. I would say he was the most influential man in Carl's life in those years. He's the one who saw something in Carl we didn't know was there.

Carl had a drive in him to do something, but he didn't know what it was. W. T. spotted it and asked Carl to become the national director for his organization. At first Carl refused, saying he was a pastor and not a traveling man. However, W. T. regularly prodded and challenged Carl and soon Carl was busy setting up offices all over the world. He didn't know he had it in him. W. T. saw it and gave him an opportunity to develop it—and Carl's been doing it ever since.

Carl would leave on Sunday night or Monday morning and would come home on Friday. One time when he came home, I said to him, "Honey, you know what I'd miss the most if something were to happen to you?" I'm usually not the humorist but when he asked what, I said, "Your little visits." He laughed until he cried, but it was true. He wasn't home much except on weekends.

He still pastored the church, so it was just a couple of days here or there when he was at home. Even so, the church continued to grow as did the child sponsorship work Carl was doing. I ran the Albuquerque office with eight people for that ministry for several years. I did all the paperwork and handled the transferring of items to the children from their sponsors.

Carl always told me I have an international face that fits in anywhere. When he pastored in Tarpon Springs, Florida, people thought I was Greek. We'd be walking down the street in the Greek community, when some people would speak to me in Greek. I would say, "I'm sorry. I don't speak Greek." One time a woman walked away saying how terrible it was that Greek girls were marrying Americans and then were ashamed of their language. We laughed but I had no idea what they were saying! When I was among Native Americans, some thought I was of the Cherokee tribe. I found I had great rapport with everybody wherever we were and maybe that was a part of the Lord's preparation for my life's work.

When we were working for W. T., we moved to Tulsa for the first time but I didn't work in the office there. To occupy my time, I bought a daycare center in Catoosa and I ran that. We weren't there very long before I sold it and we moved back to Albuquerque. Carl worked for W. T. for a short time and then worked for Don Stewart. When we were in Albuquerque, I bought another big daycare center. My work in those years was with the kiddies.

Then we moved to Phoenix so Carl could serve Don Stewart but I did not work for him at that time. Then we moved back to Santa Fe, New Mexico to be with the Assembly of God church there. After we moved back to Phoenix to work with Don again, I did work in his office during Carl's second stint there.

In Santa Fe, we had a Christian school and I taught in that. We put on a lot of musicals and music productions, like churches usually do at Christmas and other holidays. Those productions were part of the elementary children's arts and music program. The whole school was involved in all the productions. I had a wonderful assistant who was a professional and did all of the staging and handled all the production details. He was a blessing and we were able to put on some significant performances.

When Carl resigned from the church in Santa Fe, we came to Tucson and pastored First Assembly Church there. That was interesting because it's where we had met and married and there we were returning to pastor the church. That didn't last long for no sooner had I moved there after the school year was over when Carl resigned and went back to work for Don Stewart for the second time. That's when I worked with them also. Believe it or not, we were not finished with our transitions.

From Phoenix, we went back to Santa Fe to the church he had pastored the first time we lived there. That pastor, who was a good friend of Carl's, had an accident and died so we went back there to take that church. It was just a temporary sort of arrangement. This man and his wife along with Carl and I were the people who had founded LifeLink. That's where LifeLink and LifeLink International both started.

When Carl went back to Tulsa for the second time to work with Buddy Harrison and FCF, he resigned from LifeLink International, the branch that was the church but stayed on the board of the humanitarian ministry. In Tulsa, I didn't work in the office. At that time, I was caregiver for my parents who lived with us for a while and that is where we met Reggies Wenyika.

Carl was quite unhappy after Buddy Harrison passed away. Actually, we had our home up for sale when they finally let him go, so we were already trying to sell it—but it wasn't quite time. As soon as it was the Lord's time, we sold it immediately. We had it up for sale for a year before that and had never even shown it. Then in God's timing, we sold it. He knew when we needed to do it and that freed us to move back to Tucson.

Every place we went and served was a new experience with new excitement. I cried when we left Mescalero and both Native American works simply because I loved the people and hated to say goodbye. I knew if we saw them again, our relationship would be different and not as deep. They would have a new pastor and would need to respond and relate to him. That part of the transition bothered me, but the rest that came with all the moves and new positions was part of life serving the Lord.

When we returned to Tucson and FCCI began, Carl was very fulfilled and it was satisfying for me to see my husband so happy and engaged in his work. He came into his own and the people received him so well. It was a very exciting season in his life. We had people regularly coming to Tucson to visit us and I traveled with him on his trips more than I had previously.

Our most difficult trip we ever took and one I will never forget was to the Philippines. We traveled and stayed up in the mountain in the pastor's home. There was no electricity, bathrooms, or other conveniences. It was a challenge for me as a woman to go an entire week without washing my hair or taking a shower. My husband could take the bucket down, get some water, and then use the outside bathroom. Once when he took his shirt off to bathe, he heard some noise and looked over to see a row of kids watching. They wanted to know if he was "white" all the way down his body.

It rained a lot while we were there. We arrived at night but they were ready for church and were meeting in a facility with no electricity. We thought people hadn't arrived yet because the building was dark, but when they got the generator up and running and turned on the lights, the church was full. It was about nine or 10 p.m. and even though we had just arrived, we had to stay and have church with them.

Carl was always effective as he locked onto the local life or lifestyle wherever he went. He was always effective and the people loved him. He tried to take others with him so they could help with the ministry and enjoy what he was experiencing as he worked with many different people.

It may sound romantic that often we were living by faith with no set income, but believe me, it wasn't. I especially remember the lean times when we were in Mescalero. We had about $50 a month to live on and from that we had to pay rent and all other expenses. I went for groceries once a month because that's the only time we got our check—whatever amount we got. As I went down the aisles at the grocery store with my list, I first priced how much everything was and added it up. Often I had to return something to the shelf because I had gone over the amount of money I had to spend. It was tough. Sometimes we'd hear a knock at the door and were surprised to find a bag of groceries even though the donor had departed.

And now that the day has arrived to turn the responsibility over to someone else, it is quite special to see. My husband has prayed for this day and had thoughts over the years that this one or that one was to succeed him. Now that the Lord has selected Reggies, we couldn't be happier.

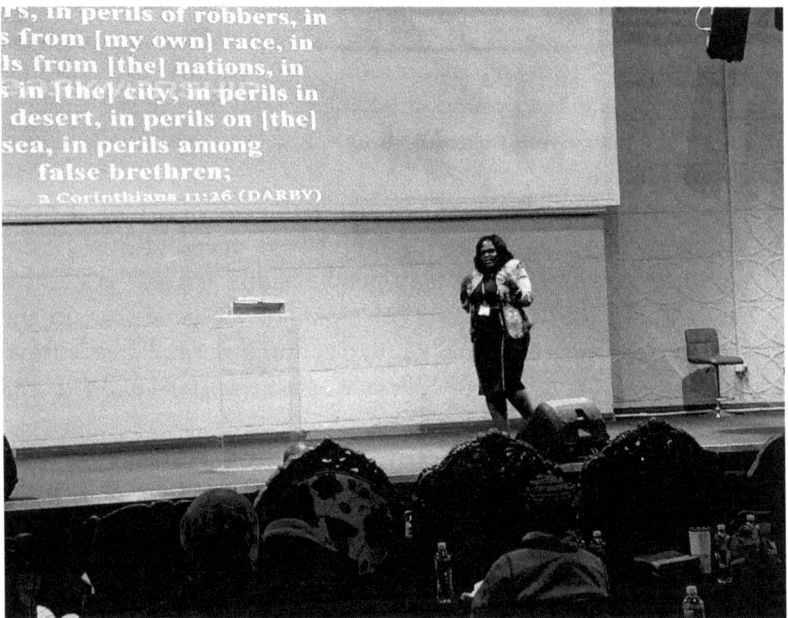

Apostle Priscilla Mgala addresses the conference in Johannesburg in 2019.

# CHAPTER THREE

# The Transition

*Dr. Carl*

Let me start this chapter by sharing the letter I drafted that contained the plan to transition FCCI'S leadership to Reggies. Then I will let him tell you more about his journey that brought him to me and to us. But first, here is part of the letter:

THE LORD HAS SPOKEN TO ME THROUGH THIS PASSAGE IN EXODUS.

MY ROLE IN FCCI NEEDS TO CHANGE VERY SOON

And it came to pass on the morrow, that Moses sat to judge the people: and the people stood by Moses from the morning unto the evening. And when Moses' father-in-law saw all that he did to the people, he said, What is this thing that thou doest to the people? Why sittest thou thyself alone, and all the people stand by thee from morning unto evening?

And Moses said unto his father-in-law, Because the people come unto me to enquire of God: When they have a matter, they come unto me; and I judge between one and another, and I do make them know the statutes of God, and his laws.

And Moses' father-in-law said unto him, the thing that thou doest is not good. Thou wilt surely wear away, both thou, and this people that is with thee: for this thing is too heavy for thee; thou art not able to perform it thyself alone.

Hearken now unto my voice, I will give thee counsel, and God shall be with thee: Be thou for the people to God-ward, that thou mayest bring the causes unto God: And thou shalt teach them ordinances and laws, and shalt shew them the way wherein they must walk, and the work that they must do. Moreover thou shalt provide out of all the people able men, such as fear God, men of truth, hating covetousness; and place such over them, to be rulers of thousands, and rulers of hundreds, rulers of fifties, and rulers of tens: And let them judge the people at all seasons: and it shall be, that every great matter they shall bring unto thee, but every small matter they shall judge: so shall it be easier for thyself, and they shall bear the burden with thee. If thou shalt do this thing, and God command thee so, then thou shalt be able to endure, and all this people shall also go to their place in peace.

So Moses hearkened to the voice of his father-in-law, and did all that he had said (Exodus 18:13–24).

I believe I have heard from the Lord, that it is time for adjustment of roles to move FCCI into its next phase. The following might be one way to approach the change:

### 1. Reggies should be named President

I selected Reggies as my successor after much prayer, and the elders have supported him as the future leader of the organization. It is time to make the transition. This would give Reggies the freedom to develop FCCI with his tremendous leadership ability. He would assume all responsibilities of president of this organization. The upcoming International Conference would be completely under his direction.

### 2. Carl will move to Vice President, Chief Operating Officer (COO)

This would allow me to be active in service to the

fellowship in ways that I am able, continuing to position the organization for success. As you know, my heart is in the field, but my physical ability and wisdom of me engaging in international travel cannot be assumed. As I see it, the COO role would include encompass the following items:

a. Support Reggies as president.

- mentor and transfer knowledge to Reggies to assist him in the transition
- be available to the president to assist him in any way possible as he assumes this new role
- provide regular reports to the President on all areas of responsibility

b. Financial management

- lead fundraising for the upcoming International Conference
- maintain donor and mailing lists, domestic and international
- receive and manage donations for FCCI and supported missionaries
- assure all financial matters, commitments, records, state and federal reports etc. are completed in a timely manner
- manage the credential process and renewals and maintain records of same
- encourage our donor list and churches to support the work of FCCI on a regular basis to provide more funding for operations and mission outreach.

c. Service and leadership for member ministers

- as my health allows, visit and encourage domestic churches to grow this area of our ministry which provides the base of our support

- provide legal services to our domestic and international leaders as needed
- provide organizational assistance to our FCCI family as needed
- Be available for travel in the U.S. for church visits, fellowship days, etc.
- communication and service to our ministers and churches as needed
- provide service to church plants as needed
- encourage young men and women to move toward ministry and support their efforts.

### 3. Teaching through technology

Through the available technology and the printed page, I can continue to speak into the lives of our ministers and leaders.

- At the request of Elder Solomon Mwesige, I am now recording a weekly video teaching that is being aired by Solomon's Christian Television Station to the entire nation of Uganda. These teachings could be put on the FCCI website as a resource for our Pastors and leaders.

- Create new video teachings and communications to provide training and impart wisdom to our pastors and leaders.

- Write a regular blog for the website to encourage, inspire and instruct our leaders.

- Create event-specific video messages that could be sent to any national or international meeting conducted by any of our churches. They could be a full 30-minute message or a shorter version depending on what is needed.

### 4. Elders move into greater roles

Our elders must assume a more active supervisory role.

That would require them to provide funding for their efforts. How that would be structured would be worked out within the group as led by the president. All needed changes would be under the leadership of Reggies. I feel it is important that elders be involved in the ministries in their region of service.

- I also feel strongly that our pastors and leaders should contribute to the support of ministries outside of their own organizational local ministry.

- Since some of our elders are aging, it is important that the elders begin to create a succession plan and begin growing their replacements.

I shared earlier how this plan unfolded over the years that followed. Now, let's hear from Reggies and let him fill in the gaps from his perspective.

★★★★★

### Dr. Reggies

I want to be clear that my involvement with Carl predates FCCI and goes back to when he was working in FCF. When Carl made his transition out of FCF, we gathered together and he shared the vision he had for starting FCCI. We gathered at Sharon Scarff's house, and Carl brought a few individuals and we all listened to his plan. Then Carl ordained us and I was among the first group to be ordained through the newly formed FCCI.

Shortly after that meeting, Carl moved to Tucson, and a year later we had our first camp meeting as we called them at the time. At that point, to be honest, I was just a nobody. I was a gopher. I was the guy who came in early before the camp meeting to help welcome all the guests. I drove to the airport to pick up some people. Then at the hotel, I would stand in the lobby, welcoming people and making sure everybody was where they needed to be. I would work with the local team, whether it was in a church or a group of volunteers. I never preached or even got the microphone to make an announcement, but I was content. It felt like home.

I would sit in the back at the meetings and that was about

it. I did that for many years, but it didn't bother me at all. People always knew that when they came to FCCI and flew in from another country, they had better be sure to have my number. That way we could connect at the airport or during the event in case they needed anything, whether it was information, a ride, or a toothbrush.

I was happy in that role. For some conferences, my entire family would drive with me just to attend the meetings. Once in a while, I would go to the office to help answer emails, make calls, or confirm arrangements with people. That's how I got to meet all the FCCI leaders and members—by being the point person for our international visitors.

Then in 2009 we had a conference someplace other than Tucson in Roanoke, Virginia. That's where Carl asked me if I could arrive early since he had duties in his church on Sunday and could not get there until Monday. I was glad to do that not just because I loved FCCI but also because Carl had been kind to me. Let me explain a little bit about why I am so grateful for Carl Conley.

## OUR VISA

When I came to the U.S., I was on a non-immigrant student visa but was in desperate need of an immigration visa. An organization based in Pittsburgh, Pennsylvania had promised to help me with this but they never followed through. All I needed was a letter of sponsorship since I carried my ordination credentials from that church. I was not asking for money, ministry, or anything else.

The letter just needed to say that this man is one of ours and belongs to our group. The group debated and hesitated, and then finally said, "We are not going to do that for you." I was bewildered for we had a ministry relationship at the time but that was it and I had no other option—or so I thought. That's when I met Carl Conley. He asked me if I needed anything, so I boldly asked if he could help me and he didn't flinch. He said, "All right, no problem. Let's apply for a religious worker's visa." From there, he handled all the paperwork and sent in the application.

In 2004 when I applied for a religious worker's visa,

immigration officials actually went to verify my existence and role, interviewing several people at Faith Community Church in Tucson. This was immediately after the September 11, 2001 terrorist attack and foreign visitors were subjected to increased and intense scrutiny. The U.S. Government wanted to make sure we were legitimate and that the organization actually existed and had the means to follow through with the sponsorship. They came to the church where Carl had set up an office for me. After they looked around and talked to some people, I got my religious worker's visa. That visa is good for two years and from there, Carl suggested we apply for a permanent resident green card. He assisted with the process and the application was submitted in 2006.

The green card process was different than the religious worker's visa and took much longer. While we were in limbo waiting for a green card, the U.S. immigration department issued my wife and me work permits so we could work. At first, my wife, Bongi, decided she was going to work for Walgreens but that changed and in 2007 she got a position with Voice of the Martyrs where she could use her journalism background. We moved from Broken Arrow, Oklahoma where we were living to Bartlesville, Oklahoma. We were still waiting for our green cards and while we were waiting, we were virtually grounded. All my international travel was shut down completely so I was unable to leave the country. I had invitations from India and every year from Australia, but I could not go until my immigration status was finalized.

Then early in 2008, I received a letter from U.S. immigration authorities stating their intent to deny my green card application. That meant they were going to send us out of the country. Carl Conley has two law degrees so when he heard of their decision, his immediate response was, "I'm going to take the government to task over this." He contacted a U.S. senator for a letter of support and prepared to go to court to fight the government on our behalf. Carl filed several documents and once again, all we could do was wait.

In May of 2008, while I was preparing to travel to Tucson to preach at Faith Community Church with Pastor Bruce Brock, I knew I could also use the visit to strategize with Carl on the way forward regarding our immigration case. I decided to check our mailbox one more time before we left for Arizona and, lo and behold, there in the mail were our green cards. The day was May 28, 2008.

From the very beginning, I knew I had found a spiritual home and the place where I belonged with Carl and FCCI. One of the worst feelings a human being can ever have is not physical pain, but the feeling of being lonely and unwanted. I had done everything I could to belong to other organizations because I thought I had something to give and wanted to make a contribution.

Even though I wasn't looking for anything, those groups made it clear they were not interested in my membership. One such group was Faith Christian Fellowship (FCF), but at least they had the courtesy of calling me to suggest I leave their organization and follow Carl Conley. They recommended I move on and I did.

My personality thrives on relationships, so I had no intention of ever leaving anybody until I found I had to. When I left FCF, I wasn't leaving to join FCCI. I was following Carl Conley to come and serve him. He had made a home for me with FCCI and made my religious worker's visa possible, then my green card. That is how I was able to carry out my ministry under the auspices of FCCI. I am obliged to give back to this organization that has enabled me to stay in the U.S.

In 2009, the FCCI elders decided to add me to their company of elders. My official title in those days, since all the elders had territories or spheres of responsibility, was "roaming elder," and that's what I did. I would roam around at our conferences or on ministry visits to serve and see how I could help others. I wasn't interested in or thinking of preaching or any leadership positions.

Then in 2012, Carl Conley wrote a letter to all the elders outlining a succession plan. He shared his vision and stated, "I need to appoint not just a vice president, but *the* vice president of both the ministry and the corporation." I knew there had been others through the years whom Carl thought would perhaps succeed him, men he had known long before I came along. I was like David when Samuel in the Old Testament went looking for the next king and to David's surprise chose him. I was that little guy at the back of the line and wasn't thinking of a role with FCCI other than the one I had.

When Carl asked me to serve as vice president, I already had a full-time job at a university. That prevented me from traveling with Carl to other parts of the world where he was going. However, I accepted the post as vice president with the understanding that one day I would be the general superintendent of FCCI. Carl then wrote his letter he shared with you earlier and sent it to all the elders, and all the elders endorsed that arrangement. And that's where we are as I write. I wasn't looking for this. That's not why I joined FCCI. In fact, when Carl first approached me, I didn't want it, but because I felt my heart was joined to Carl's, I saw myself as the guardian of what Carl started. I need to make sure it carries on and grows. That's why I accepted.

There are people who are in full-time ministry who could probably do and be more involved than I am right now, but I think what I bring to the table is the ability to strategically connect people from all over the world while ensuring they have an adequate sense of belonging. That I do well. I connect and bring people together and people feel like they have found a home. That's one of the important characteristics that comprise the FCCI ethos. Anybody who comes to be with us feels like it's a home. That's why we titled this book *A Place Called Home*.

Once I received my green card in 2008, I could then leave the country and rest assured I would actually be allowed back in. My first trip with Carl was to Bishop G. Thomas in India. I had first met Bishop G. in person in 2006. Previously, I had known about him through email and by letter. When we first met, I was fulfilling my role as host and caretaker of the international guests at the FCCI Conference. I saw a man sitting by himself, so I asked him to join me and a friend of mine from South Korea for a meal.

While at dinner, he said these words that I will never forget, "I've been sitting and watching you for two days, praying and thinking, 'I wish this man would talk to me. This man could come to my country. He is from Africa. He would understand what our lives are like.'" We broke bread and had dinner together and he invited me to come to India. At the time, I had neither the means nor the time to travel. It was not until January of 2012 when I felt like I needed to make the trip. Even though we had no money and there were many pressing obligations, I called Carl and said, "I don't know how I'm going to do this, but I want to go to India with you."

## INDIA

The weather in Oklahoma was terrible that spring season even by Oklahoma's standards. The roof on my house was damaged by hail and I needed to replace it. It was an old roof, so I knew the insurance company was not going to pay full price to replace it. It was going to cost us a lot of money. One day, I was chatting with the roofer while he was working on our roof and he asked me, "What have you got going on?"

I told him, "I need to go on a mission trip to India. I'm just trying to figure out how to put the finances together to do that."

"How much will that cost you?" When I told him that I needed $5,000, he responded, "Come to the office and we will help you with that."

When I went to his office, he wrote me a $5,000 check—just like that. I called Carl and said, "I'm in." Even with that blessing, the faculty and staff at the university where I was working collected another $3,000 along with different goods to assist our hosts and their friends in India. When everything was said and done, I ended up taking six full suitcases, weighing 50 pounds each, filled with medical supplies, feminine products, and other things for the ministry in India—along with $8,000 in cash.

Then my colleagues gathered more money for me and bought me a camera because they wanted me to send back pictures of our work there. I finally ended up traveling to an FCCI event, while also representing my colleagues at the university to whom I sent pictures and a video every day. It was a series of miracles one after the other.

For example, when I had checked in at the airport in Oklahoma City, the airline agreed to check only three bags through to India for free, but said I had to pay for the other three. I looked at the lady who was checking my bags and said, "I want you to know something. These bags are a donation. If I part with the money to pay for this, it's money I could be using to feed orphans. Talk to your manager. I don't want to pay for those bags."

She looked at me and laughed, then said, "You're crazy." I said, "Just tell your manager exactly that. Tell him there's a crazy man here asking if he can check three more bags for free." I stood there for a long time after she disappeared into the back room. When she came back, she didn't say anything to me but proceeded to put tags on the bags and threw them on the conveyor belt—at no extra charge.

When I landed in Chennai, India, my concern was how to get all six checked bags together and securely exit the airport to the people who were waiting to pick me up. Wouldn't you know it, there was a policeman in the airport who was quite abrupt with me, yelling to hurry, get my stuff, and move out of the way of the other arriving passengers. That was difficult given that I had to locate and transport six bags. I had to take one bag at a time and leave it somewhere so I could retrieve the others.

The policeman was so frustrated with me that he started grabbing my bags and throwing them on carts. That is how the Lord provided help for me, and how I was able to walk out with all my bags pushing one cart and pulling the other. No one who picked me up could figure out how one person was able to transport six bags. That was my experience going to my first international FCCI event.

We had arranged for our FCCI elder from Australia to meet us in India. Carl, who was also meeting me in Chennai on a flight from China, had been joined there by Annetta, another FCCI elder based in the Philippines. The fellowship and ministry we enjoyed together in India were fantastic. It was also some of the best preaching I've ever done—if I say so myself. I was preaching four, five, and even six times a day.

India can be a tough duty venue, however, and members of our team became sick throughout our time there. I was the only one who didn't get sick. Annetta is a trained nurse but couldn't care for anyone because she was bedridden. She was supposed to be the one handling the distribution of the feminine products and explaining to the girls how to use them. I ended up doing that, also handling the explanation for an audience of 250 girls. It was wonderful and my dark skin did a very good job hiding the degree to which I was blushing through it all.

When I got back to the U.S., I picked up my car at the airport, headed to the office to drop off the videos I had taken, and immediately had to run to the bathroom because I was sick. Though I was sick for the next two days, I was still pleased that the work had been done. That was my first taste of what's out there and how important it is. It gave me an idea of what Carl had been doing for many years, and God alone knows the price he has paid to do it.

That trip showed me the possibilities for FCCI and the needs we could help meet. We had a chance to minister to people who could never pay us back, people who hung on every word that came from our mouths. They are so grateful any time we visit to support them. When we go, they are counting on the fact that we are men and women of God who have a word from the Lord for them.

Many leaders stood for ordination at the 2019 South Africa conference.

# CHAPTER FOUR

# Moving Forward

*Dr. Reggies*

Our biggest challenge as we move forward is how to structure the work we do and opportunities we have. Obviously, I must have a job in order to make a living and support my family. The ministry doesn't have sufficient resources to support Carl, and we *will* support Carl for the rest of his life because he founded the work—it is the right thing to do. Now we must trust God that He will open doors and hearts for more revenue to come in. We don't have much overhead and that's why we've been able to do what we have done so far to help so many and reach more people.

I think people appreciate that we are not asking them to be part of something with a large administrative presence to support. They receive us as people who have joined together to help them, not expecting them to help us. We want to equip them to be better at the good things they already do. We hope they learn from us how they can adjust the things that limit their ministries or impede their growth—whether it's personal or professional. We want them to do what they do well and be able to do even more of it.

We are not what I would call "imperialistic" in any way. We don't go into places thinking we know it all, thus telling the local experts what we, the visitors, think they should do. We go into places to encourage people and ministries and give them the tools we have that will benefit them and the people they serve.

## ANNUAL MEETINGS

When we first started our annual camp meetings or conferences, they were mostly attended by our elders and some of their leaders. Then they grew so we started meeting bi-annually. While Carl was traveling and making a big impact where he went, I would say the trip to India was FCCI's first chance to make an international impact. More than 200 pastors in India showed up and those leaders had no possibility of accessing anything like we had. These pastors went back to their villages and have since been doing a tremendous work. Then in 2017 when we held our FCCI conference in Malawi, we experienced our largest gathering of people. I believe both of those are simply the first fruits of more to come.

I liked the way we structured the Malawi conference. Different people from various ministries from within FCCI preached in the morning sessions, and every afternoon we heard reports from the different ministries. Each region or each person prepared a report that told people, "Here's what we've done since we were last together." They could use a video, PowerPoint, or whatever else they had to help make their presentation. We had two or three such reports every day.

Ordination has always been a part of our conferences. We are not a denomination, but we realize that in some countries, proof as to the legitimacy of ministry credentials is important. We felt people needed to know that once they joined our fellowship, ministry credentialing was something we were willing to oversee and provide. We don't do it so we can grow our membership; we are not an ordination service. We do it as a tool to serve, equip, and empower our members for ministry in their respective nations.

We also do it to recognize that these people are called into the ministry and often are already accomplished ministers. When they agree to be ordained by FCCI, they are saying, "I'd like to be part of this fellowship, not only for what I can get out from it, but also for what I'm able to bring to the table to encourage others who are part of it."

We only agree to ordain people we know or who are known by our elders. If they are recommended by one of our elders from their country or region, then they can participate. The elders must be able to vouch for their character and the viability of their ministry. They handle the interviews and training as they see fit. Then they can explain what FCCI stands for and what membership means.

It's never been our custom to invite outside speakers to the conference. It was always family addressing family. That has its benefits and drawbacks. It can be a drawback because our members may not always be proficient or experienced in certain areas for which members need training. Sometimes hearing from the same people can result in circulating the same ideas, unless the people are professional, called, and competent ministry trainers who do that for a living. The benefit is that we get to hear from one another and know how to pray and support what is being done—and also get new ideas we can pursue further because we know those who are doing it. We can then write or even visit them to learn more.

Our conferences are self-funded. As mentioned earlier, we solicit pledges from our members and then collect offerings. We make sure that the next conference is paid for by pledges and offerings from the previous one —and that has worked for us. Whether we keep that model for the future or not remains to be seen. We operate on a very lean budget because it's a family gathering. It needs to continue having that feel because that's the FCCI way. It's a place called home and not a business.

That's why we don't require anyone to leave the organization, fellowship, or denomination of which they already a part. In fact, we encourage them to have multiple connections and memberships. We are fine with any individual who is a member of another denomination and wants to join FCCI. They still benefit from our network and hopefully find some of the things we do that would be beneficial for them to learn.

## WHY JOIN FCCI?

Maybe you are a church leader and are thinking as you read, "Why should I join FCCI?" My question is, "Why *not* FCCI?" FCCI can serve as an additional resource supplementing the resources you already have. FCCI is not here to replace what people have, but to augment or complement whatever it is that they have. That's one of the reasons why FCCI has been as successful as it has been. FCCI is an organization that welcomes others, especially those who don't have a home organization. It's a place called home for many and I regularly hear this characterization from many people: They felt welcome. They never felt like an outsider because of our philosophy of ministry and how we approach things.

We seem to attract the people with whom most major organizations do not spend much time. Most of our pastors who I would call the end users of our materials or resources are people who can never pay for the materials or repay anyone. That fact has never discouraged us whereas most major organizations would find that approach to ministry not to be sustainable. We made up our minds that we will never stop this as we go into different nations.

We welcome pastors from the village, pastors who don't speak English, leaders who might not have a pair of shoes. Because they are pastors and are preaching, whether to a congregation of 15, or 150, or 1,500, meeting under a tree or in a dilapidated building, we consider them a legitimate part of the workforce of the Kingdom. They are our equals. We are not afraid to go where most big organizations would consider unsuitable and unsustainable. It's about people and we place the same premium on a soul regardless of socioeconomic or geographical locus.

God has given us the grace to do those things and that's why FCCI is unique. An FCCI event is the place where we expect all to show up fully prepared to contribute, at least by encouraging someone else. We are not asking that they do that from the pulpit but rather in fellowship. That's where most of the ministry takes place and that's why we always mix with everyone.

That is also why we make it a point that we all eat together. We fellowship together and there are no distinctions. It is for this reason that I am reticent to invite the so-called big-name preachers because they are notorious for expecting special treatment and may not want to sit down and eat with the pastor who has no shoes—but we do. That's our signature trait. The people coming in know they're going to rub shoulders with Carl, all the other elders, and me.

Leaders have to jump through too many hoops to be a member of some organizations but it's easy to belong to FCCI. The only hoop anyone has to jump through for FCCI is to believe in Jesus Christ and to be in need of fellowship and encouragement while being willing to share what they have and know with others. So again, my answer to the question, "Why should I join FCCI?" is "Why not FCCI?"

## THE 2019 CONFERENCE

South Africa was an impactful time for me. I wanted the official transition to take place on my home soil amongst my own people. It gave me a satisfying feeling of coming back home and including brothers and sisters from those communities, like the one in which I was raised in Zimbabwe, into the process and my journey. It was also special in that the gathering included more than just African brothers and sisters. They came from all over the world to attend the conference. That's the power of FCCI. People need an empathetic friend, one who understands their context and one who can minister to them and their followers within that context.

In FCCI, people find and relate with colleagues who have the needed versatility and cultural competence to go into their areas and not be condescending or patronizing. Rather, these colleagues actually go in respecting the culture while pointing them to Christ and giving them tools they need to continue to impact their communities. They need somebody who's able to roll up their sleeves and get their hands dirty right along with them. They need somebody who will be happy to come in and preach in the trenches and get his boots and shirt dirty.

Our FCCI elders are able and prepared to do that. They will sleep under a tree if that's what the job calls for—and we've all done it. They'll sleep in a mosquito-infested area. We've done whatever the work calls for. If you are one of those people who want to be sitting in a tall building on the eleventh floor and attempt to command the world from there, you probably are not going to find FCCI a very comfortable place.

Being back in Africa after having been gone for 20 years was surreal. Some things have moved on and changed, and some have not. What impacted me the most was how I was able to impact people because of how much God had given me in the last 20 years. I was able to return and give back. Twenty years ago when I left, I was a nobody who did not have two dimes to rub together. God has transformed me and in turn, I could return and make a transformational difference in the lives of others. He has given me a ministry and my job is now to give away ministry. He has given me an ability to connect people and create an environment where everybody feels like they belong and at home. I'm able to do that effortlessly. That's what I take to the nations as I bring people together. It made me happy and fulfilled.

South Africa was the closest I've gotten to my home country since I left. But then again, you could say I have no home country. I live in the United State where I am a citizen, but every community that is similar to the one I came from is just as easily my home. I have no qualms about it. In Santa Cruz, Bolivia, I felt at home, in Barranquilla, Colombia, I once again felt at home. The same is true of Tenali in Andhra Pradesh, India—and the list could go on.

## THE TRANSITION

The FCCI leadership transition from Dr. Carl to me is an ongoing process that was ushered in by what the elders did in South Africa. Obviously, Carl is still around and for that, we rejoice. Carl is still the head elder and continues to exercise and wield spiritual authority. I was vested with all authority but I chose to give some of it back to him. From here, we need to recruit more people to come alongside and help us take this work to other parts of the world.

My job is to reproduce myself in other people and ministries. My hope is that those who are impacted by our efforts will do the same for others. I am bi-vocational so FCCI is not my full-time job and I do not receive any compensation from the ministry whatsoever. Therefore, I have to be a bit more strategic about this next phase. As far as leadership goes, we are going to bring in a new crop of leadership and reach out to some younger people and leaders. Then we will give them a reason to see FCCI as a place where they too can belong and call home as I have done for many years. We will trust God for the resources to help them.

Therefore, I hope the next phase is a growth phase, even though the pandemic slowed down everything in ministry to a crawl for some and, sadly, a standstill for others. Now that we are emerging from our lockdowns, I want to be more intentional. Let's measure our growth and let's hold ourselves accountable to the Lord for the resources we have and see if we are making a measurable and documentable difference. Are we winning or making an impact beyond just anecdotal information and testimonies from people? Are we actually making an impact and moving the needle in the right direction for the Kingdom of God?

I would like to see more women in leadership as well as speakers and trainers at our conferences or gatherings. I want men and women to come into an FCCI event and see people who look like them and be able to identify with them and build relationships. It's important for people to come into a place and say, "Glory to God, people like us are welcome here."

## EXPECTATIONS

As the general superintendent, I speak for all of us when I outline the following expectations. First, we expect people to come into this fellowship to encourage others and share what they have and what they know. After all, it is better to give than to receive. We're not talking about money, but about ministry. I know ministry takes money and we absolutely must have it, but ministry is first and foremost about people.

Second, we expect people to grow personally and professionally as a result of their participation in our ministry. FCCI is not for the people who think they have arrived. Third, we expect people to support our work. I don't draw a salary from FCCI so when I stand up and say, "Support the work," I'm talking about supporting FCCI's ability to deploy assistance, ministry training, and networking opportunities to brothers and sisters located in the four corners of the world. We expect people to shoulder the financial responsibility of reaching out to others by cultivating a "giver" mentality and spirit and not a "taker" one.

And finally, we want our members to learn from and love one another. We're going to have differences of ministry philosophy and tactics, but that's not the main thing that holds us together. As long as someone believes in the Lordship of Jesus Christ, and as long as they believe and know the Bible is the inspired Word of God and choose to live and conduct their lives in Bible-honoring manner, they are welcome to the fellowship.

Later in the book, I unpack these expectations further, but I thought it would be good for you to hear from some of the other FCCI elders and members so they could briefly describe their own spiritual journey that led them to us and brought us together. Then after you hear from Enrique, Pastor Louise, Priscilla, Ebenezer, and George, Carl and I will come back and close out this book with some concluding thoughts.

Bishop Levy Silindza's church was the host for the South Africa conference

# CHAPTER FIVE

# Let's Hear from the Members

*I (Reggies) thought it would be good for you to hear from some of our FCCI members to learn why they joined FCCI, what they have gained from their membership, and where they think the organization is headed.*

★★★★★

## Dr. Felix Omobude
*Founder of Gospel Light International Ministries, Benin City, Nigeria*

Before I founded Gospel Light Ministries in 1988, I worked with the well-known Bishop in Nigeria, Benson Idahosa, for 13 years. While I was with Bishop Idahosa, probably in 1982, Pastor Louise Brock was invited to come and speak to the church network of which I was a part. She came as part of a team with Daisy Osborne. It was Pastor Louise who introduced me to FCF, which is where I met Dr. Carl Conley. As I built a relationship with Dr. Carl, I saw a sincere man, hungry for God, passionate about the Kingdom.

I think Pastor Louise saw the local challenges I was facing and knew I needed relationships to help me grow. I needed exposure to new things and ideas. At that time, I had finished my training at Christ for the Nations in the U.S. and before returning home, she felt it would be good for me to meet with the head of FCF, Buddy Harrison, I also visited Pastor Louise's storefront church and our relationship continued to blossom—and it is still strong today.

Pastor Louise visited Nigeria a few more times and I also attended a few FCF conferences. To be completely honest, and many of the international members of FCF would agree with me, it was Dr. Carl who served us all passionately and selflessly, and that meant so much to me and to all of us. I continued to build a relationship with Dr. Carl, who has been to Nigeria a number of times. I would take him around with me and he has even been to the village where I was born. Of course, I've taken him to some of our network churches within and outside the country.

I can remember when FCCI started. We were attending an FCF conference and visiting in Carl Conley's hotel room. I stated that most of us internationals came because of Dr. Carl. If he ever left FCF, I asked what we were going to do. Interestingly enough, that is what happened. Dr. Carl left and we all had to make a decision whether we were going to stay in FCF or follow Dr. Carl.

Honestly, the mission of my church and organization is to impact our world for the better, not to build an organization or hierarchy. I needed people with a like mind. In my own view, Carl Conley had served very selflessly. He demanded nothing. He's a father figure to many. For eight years, I led the Pentecostals in Nigeria so I know the kinds of problems pastors face. I know the challenges. Carl Conley has become the father figure to many because he met and helped us where we were, and did not use us to build his own ministry. He helped others build theirs. I have been part of organizations and then left them because they existed only to take resources from its members or to maintain the status quo. I was not and am not interested in groups like that, which is why I am still a part of FCCI—and always will be. FCCI gives and doesn't take.

When I heard Dr. Carl was starting his own organization, I encouraged him and told him I would participate. The fact that Pastor Louise and Pastor Bruce were a part was only more of an incentive for me to be involved, for I knew and respected them. I came to their first meeting in Tucson and it was there that we talked about how to finance future meetings.

I know money plays a major role in every organization's

existence, so I encouraged those present to commit a certain amount to help fund the next conference. The people responded and now it is a part of every one of our meetings. We don't leave until we have raised the money for our next conference, and I am glad to play a part in that. I teach our people in Nigeria to be responsible and generous with the opportunities we have. I could do no less as a member of FCCI.

I learned in the early years of my ministry the value of relationships. What FCCI has brought to me, my churches, and my country could not be purchased with money. We have heard speakers and a deposit of the Spirit flows into us. I belong to a family. If anything were to happen, I have strong people I can call for help. That means a lot to me. FCCI has certainly played an important role.

As church leaders, many look up to us. They don't think we have any pain but when they are in pain, they come to us. I have found in FCCI that I can come and pour out my heart. If I need a friend, they are there to share tears with me if I need that. If I'm happy, they rejoice with me. We serve as a covering to each other. If at any time someone feels I'm going off course, I would hope they would have the courage to bring it to my attention and say, "We don't think that's the right thing to do." There are security and safety in that.

Now we are at a time when there needs to be a leadership transition. We all knew that one day Dr. Carl was not going to be able to do the things he used to do. We spent some time together when he spoke to me about it. We prayed and looked around at who was in our midst to assume leadership. We knew the Lord was leading us to Dr. Reggies. He has my total support and blessing. It is even more special that he is an African brother.

Some African leaders I know don't even go near to others or allow others to get near to talk to them. Dr. Reggies' heart is right. He grew up in the FCCI vision and is aware of what we stand for. He knows I can call him if he is not walking straight. I sent my son to be with him to study and Dr. Reggies took him in as his own son, as family. I'm very proud of him. My prayers are with him.

If you are reading this and considering being part of FCCI, I would encourage you to consider the value of being involved in a global Kingdom assignment. As we walk together, we can teach one another, rebuke when necessary and direct when necessary if someone fails. Dr. Reggies has a fine group of people around him who have been tried and tested. FCCI is a very good resource and Dr. Reggies represents and mirrors through his own personal life what we stand for. I think if FCCI focuses on service to the Kingdom, we will do well. FCCI is marshalling the spiritual resources available to it with the aim of using them to advance the Kingdom.

What to eat, where to sleep, or what to drive are not my problems. God has blessed me. However, I am aware that there are many people out there who love God but whose houses are a wreck. They want to do their best but they are constrained. We need to encourage them and help them out. I got a call recently from a young lad who went to our school some years ago. He now lives in Canada. He called to remind me how I offered him a scholarship. Those are the kinds of stories that refresh my life. That is what FCCI needs to be doing—helping others reach their full potential in Christ. If we do that, then we will expand to many nations of the world because we will be known for our service, for what we can give, and not what we can get or take. That is important to keep in mind as we move forward. I am confident we will.

I also hope we will be mindful of our founder, Dr. Carl. Dr. Reggies has assured me Dr. Carl will be taken care of and I think that is important. We must give our leaders wherever they are an opportunity to support him. You don't get out of poverty by prayer or fasting. You have to give. We have to teach people how to survive and then thrive, instead of trying to feed them—they need to learn how to feed themselves as they carry out their own Kingdom assignment.

★★★★★

*Anne Wood*
*Founder and President*
*Life Solutions in Abundance International Inc.*

I spent many years in China, mostly as a humanitarian

worker among some church people there. I never went to the underground church because I was too visible and thus the government knew me too well. My first year there, I volunteered in the Guangdong Christian Council close to Hong Kong. That made me a marked woman, so to speak, but that was okay because God had His plan there for me.

After 13 years, the security issue was dangerous for the person with whom I worked closely because they often shielded me from the police. When the authorities finally came to my house and my associate was not able to stay there while they searched, we knew it was time for me to leave for it wasn't safe any longer. When I was ready to leave, I asked God where He wanted me to go and He said, "Go to Asia."

It took me a year to get out of China as I was traveling to different places while I was seeking God. I went to India, Malaysia, and Singapore but didn't feel like I was supposed to go to any of those. Then I came to the States to attend a missions conference and met a doctor from the Philippines who invited me to come and visit his hospital.

I went to visit and when I drove into the town, I knew it was the place. It was San Fernando La'union. There are two cities named San Fernando that are north of Manila. The first one's close to Manila, but the one I went to is farther away. By expressway we are about four and a half hours from Manila, but we used to be about nine or ten hours by bus so it's getting easier to travel there. In the fall of 2021, I will have been there for 13 years, equal to the amount of time I was in China.

God has never been clear to me about what I was going to do when I told Him I would go wherever He sent me. Some people know what to do, but they don't know where to go, but mine's been the other way. I knew where to go but wasn't always clear about what I was to do. I had to wait and develop that after I arrived. Since I didn't know what to do, I just started serving those God brought my way who had needs. I started a women's ministry and a group for Bible school students. Soon a young pastor was asking me to come to his program's anniversary celebrations and graduations so I built relationships there.

Over the years I have developed a team of 10 co-workers. We built a library with 2,000 books and we did mobile library work out into the mountains. We did children's ministry around that as well. We always had batches of kids for every mobile outreach. Then we did movie evangelism. We had a livelihood project for women that focused on jewelry making.

Then about four years ago, God gave me a vision of a target. I've never been big on visions, so when that happens to me, it gets my attention. The target was full of arrows except the bull's-eye was empty. I looked at that and asked, "What does that mean?" The impression I got was that it represented the Philippine Church. There was lots of good work, but they were missing the bull's-eye.

I reasoned, "Oh, but they're doing evangelism there. They're winning souls." It was true they were reaching the unsaved but not the unreached people groups of the nation. It's amazing how many people don't understand the difference between those two groups—the unsaved and the unreached. I had to learn and re-understand what I thought I knew about the Great Commission.

I learned I really didn't know very much. I think most people assume they understand the Great Commission which means He will touch all the people groups of the world with the gospel of Jesus Christ. We will not forever be going on missions. He intends to complete it, and I think He wants this generation to be the completing generation.

The Philippine Church has heard prophecies that it would send many missionaries out to the nations and they are in hearty agreement whenever that is said or talked about. The problem is they don't quite know how to accomplish the task. Now I understand God has raised me up to help mobilize the Philippine church to embrace and fulfill their portion of the Great Commission.

My ministry is a fully registered ministry in the Philippines. When I'm gone, the ministry will belong completely to them and will be run by citizens of the Philippines. We're well into that transition now. There is one young woman who is 32 as I write but has been with me for 10 years. She's just starting to make decisions and is ready and willing to take more responsibility, which means I can take on a different role that does not involve so much of the day-to-day operations. However, I'm still wearing several hats and one is a coordinator for a missions movement among the local churches of which there are Nazarene, Presbyterian, Baptist, Independent Baptist, Pentecostal, Independent, and the Mission Movement churches.

It's become a dynamic thing because we're working to direct that movement, which involves church planting, into un-reached people groups. The Philippines alone has 32 unreached people groups and 14 Muslim unreached people groups. Those groups do not have a viable presence of a church or a gospel herald among them, which is remarkable today. The Philippine Mission Association, with whom we are working as partners, is targeting those 14 Muslim groups right now so we are organizing lots of prayer meetings as well as training sessions.

I am also the coordinator for the Colorado group named AIMS for the northern Philippines. I'm a certified trainer and coordinator for that organization. As I write, I just completed tak-ing 42 pastors from three provinces through a strategic missions course in three provinces using Zoom technology. I followed up three weeks later from the States via Zoom. Those pastors are beginning to raise up young people to do the work of the church so they, the pastors, can go out and do missionary work. It's quite exciting to see it emerge and for me to be a part of it through training and equipping.

My other major work these days is in Pakistan. I didn't have much interest in Pakistan. All I knew is it was a country by India until I started meeting many Pakistanis. In 2017, I had met two Pakistanis, one being in the Philippines as a missionary. Then when I went to Thailand later that year, I met four other Pakistanis there. The missionary is now a part-time staff member for me. Then another one I met got us fully registered in Pakistan so we're a totally indigenous ministry there now. We're not bound to them other than to do consulting and helping them when we can. Nevertheless, they're responsible for our ministry there. It's amazing because they have a book translation and distribution project and they are investigating translating and distributing one of my books. They've already started a women's ministry and in the first half of 2021, they planted 10 churches.

My connection with FCCI began when I was in China. Darlene, my ministry partner there, belonged to a church in Missouri and Terry, their pastor, had a relationship with Carl Conley. Darlene happened to be in the church when Pastor Terry went to the trash can, pulled out a piece of paper, and said, "I think I'll go to this meeting in Hong Kong and meet up with Carl." After he said that, Darlene faxed that announcement to me and I decided I would go. It was a 24-hour train trip to get there back then and while I was on my way there, they changed the meeting venue. When I got there, I couldn't find them.

However, a man who had gone to the first meeting was staying in the same guest house as I was but he couldn't go to the second one. When he learned who I was, he said, "Carl Conley's looking for you" and that's how I got to the meeting and eventually connected with Carl when he was part of FCF. That would have been 1996.

When I met Carl, I'd been in a certain ministry fellowship but I was always the outsider. My hair was too short, I was female, I was alone, and I was divorced. They were lovely people, but I wasn't jelling with them. When I met Carl, we talked and before the meeting was over, he said, "Next time you're home, come to Tulsa and see me." I did and we just hooked up.

At that point, I was quite isolated in China. I was one of the first people to use the internet in the town. Believe me when I say Carl was there for me every day. Sometimes it would require 20 minutes to get a simple email sent, but he always responded and helped me feel connected to a group with a like mind and mission. He is one of two people who, had they not been in my life, I probably would not have made it through those early, isolated days I spent in China.

However, things did not come together for me as part of FCF. I didn't find the support was what I'd expected from that kind of an organization. The only real support that came was when we did a well project in China. Carl went to one of the conferences and raised some money, but as far as ongoing relationships with them, to this day I really have few contacts with anyone in that organization. Carl was where my connection was.

When I came back to the States after that, Carl was getting ready to have the first FCCI meeting. Many of his international friends had said they were going stay with him. When we had that first meeting at Bruce Brock's church, I walked in and Carl saw me, pulled me into a side room, and informed me, "You're going to be one of my elders in FCCI" and that's how I served from that point forward. He had been such a blessing to me that I wasn't about to say I couldn't do that.

I have never been sorry I stayed with Carl. I've done what I can for FCCI. I recruited the first Pakistani pastors, and now we have seven Pakistanis who are part of FCCI. In 2021, we ordained two more in the Philippines. We now have seven in the Philippines. I've not pushed to make that happen, it just did.

FCCI has been a stabilizing force in my life and ministry since day one. It's not been a burden in any way. It's the place God has put me. I believe I belong here. It's home. I don't see changing any of that. I do belong to another organization in the Philippines, Kingsway Fellowship International, based in Des Moines. They've done very well in the Philippines.

The reason I joined them was initially I needed a ministry covering and they let me function under their umbrella. We still have a good relationship. When I'm able to do something with them, I do. They often invite me to speak at their big conferences, but my first obligation or first commitment is FCCI. Now that Dr. Reggies is taking over as general superintendent, I am optimistic about the future. Everyone loves Reggies and sees God's hand on his life. I'm perfectly supportive of Dr. Reggies and think he's God's appointed person.

If you are reading this book and considering FCCI, I assure you that you will find spiritual mentorship when you need it. God will provide advice, fellowship, and opportunities through the partnerships you will form within this community of believers from all over the world. Are there obligations? I don't see any of it as being an obligation but rather more of a privilege. With my limited budget, I support the conferences every month. Otherwise, it would be difficult to make any financial commitment in one lump-sum payment. We've done that for several years and I've always been blessed. It's not a burden. God has always provided.

When I think back to my FCF days, I felt a pull for money that was gut wrenching. I either felt ashamed I couldn't do more or sometimes felt abandoned because I could not. I don't think FCCI will ever get that attitude toward the people it serves.

I hope we do a better job of networking with one another over the coming years and not just among leadership. Members need to set up networks through which they can connect. Of course, now with Zoom and other technology, it's never been easier to do. I'm now part of a network out of Canada that started less than two years ago, and they're already in 45 nations with over 500 in membership. They asked me to be an advisor to the women. I've been doing that as I am able, but it's not my primary focus. For my remaining years as God provides the strength, I want to do what I can to help FCCI be part of the Great Commission as I understand it today.

★★★★★

*Rev. Enrique Figueroa pastor at Templo Calvario*
*Camino al Tecnologico, Fracc. Los Naranjos*
*Navojoa, Sonora, Mexico*

My name is Enrique Figeroa and I have been the pastor at Templo Calvario in Navojoa, Sonora, Mexico for 38 years. A missionary from the U.S. planted the church and then I became the pastor. I am not bi-vocational so I have been blessed to be a full-time pastor all these years. I met Dr. Carl Conley at an FCCI missions conference. I was drawn to FCCI because of its heart for missions and I have not been disappointed. At that event, I met leaders from India, Tanzania, Nigeria, and many other countries. I felt at home and my heart was so happy.

When I invited Jesus into my heart, I desired to serve him by perhaps going to Africa or India as a missionary. However, I was working in Mexico with all my heart, but I never lost my desire to work with people in those countries. When I met Carl,

I felt like God opened the doors for me to go to these places. My first conference I went to with Dr. Carl was in Kenya. After that, he invited me to go to India. Then I went with him to Malawi. He invited me to go with him to Nicaragua. Then I went to Spain with him. I pray to God that He will open doors for me to go to other nations. This has fulfilled my dream of visiting and preaching in foreign lands. Dr. Conley and FCCI have given me an opportunity to fulfill my purpose and my dream in the Lord.

It has also been wonderful that Brother Carl visited my church and has helped me as a counselor. He is a pastor and understands the work. He has also preached here and has evangelized in my town. Many pastors are missionaries like myself and they feel alone. FCCI helps me feel like I'm part of the family or a group. It's never about what they can get. It's about what they can give me.

Even though the pandemic has kept us apart, I am looking forward to our next meeting in Tucson. To me, it's going to be exciting to be with pastors from around the world. If I went to Malawi, I should be able to get to Tucson.

★★★★★

*Pastor Louise Brock, FCCI Founding Elder*

I've known Dr. and Mrs. Conley for a long time and actually knew Carl's mother. I was in the New Mexico District of the Assemblies of God for several years where his mother was a home missionary to some Native American tribes. I had known the family for quite some time and back then was aware of Carl's passion for missions.

Then when I was affiliated with Buddy Harrison and Faith Community Fellowship (FCF), I traveled extensively internationally. I had founded a Bible school called School of the Bible and I set one up in many foreign countries. After Buddy passed away, things in that organization changed. I thought the organization would continue with his vision, but it didn't and I'm not sure exactly why they didn't—at least in my opinion it did not.

Carl had been working with Buddy Harrison and when he was leaving it, he called and we chatted for some time about his vision and future. My son and I invited him and his family to move to Tucson. When he began Faith Community Churches

International (FCCI), we provided support and office space so he could have an engine to launch and drive his vision. He had been sort of the international representative for Buddy Harrison, so when that role ceased, the Lord led him to stay in touch with all the missionaries he had built relationships with in FCF.

In FCF, I had been active in establishing Bible schools and leadership training while Carl had been active in the pioneering of churches and mentoring pastors in different countries to become pastors—or better equipped leaders. I taught in Bible schools and seminars all over Africa and traveled millions of miles over a 14-year period. When Carl and Ellene moved to Tucson, they asked me to be a board member and also serve as one of the elders of the organization. I happily agreed and I still serve in those capacities. I have a significant interest in foreign missions, and I have worked with Carl closely for years now in FCCI.

I felt FCCI was a good way to continue the relationships Carl and I both had with ministries in Africa, the Islands, and other places all over the world. We had contacts and formed FCCI to be an American-based organization that would help leaders in other nations financially and educationally, as well as through humanitarian efforts.

We get involved in practically every kind of issue you could think of, things like sending money, lending support, and being supportive in any other way there was a need. I know FCCI has been and is a great comfort to people in foreign countries. Those of us who are Americans and consider ourselves missionaries due to our travel and connections in other nations have seen what FCCI can mean to those who are working on a foreign field. We are their safety net in the States to help them.

We are here to help them financially. We pray for them when they overextend, or get tired, or fall ill. When that happens, we're there. We fill a lot of needs. We are active all the time, staying in close contact with our partners and friends. I recently hosted Jeff Rogers from Malawi in my church. I've known him for many years and I know Dr. Reggies and Dr. Carl have known him as well. FCCI has relationships that have lasted for generations and generations. That's not common in a lot of organizations.

Carl and Ellene attend our church services and we are the best of friends. We have lunch together almost every Sunday. I never get a message from a missionary that I don't forward to him and likewise, him to me. He's comfortable with FCCI resting on the platform of this church without being totally dependent upon it. We are going to host the 2021 convention at our church.

We are deeply involved in missions and I would say have made a significant impact for a church our size. We're not a mega-church, but God has blessed us financially so we can be a blessing to others. During the COVID-19 pandemic, our finances have actually increased and for this we thank God. I am a firm believer and teacher of the principle that what you sow, you'll reap. Our FCCI churches are sowing churches. We believe if we sow into the right soil, God will abundantly bless us and our partners.

I founded Faith Community Church in 1981 originally as an Assembly of God church but now we are an independent work. From the time we started, we have kept growing and growing. Eventually, we bought property and built a bigger church with a wonderfully designed layout that enhances our ministry effectiveness. We have an office building and a sanctuary. We were running about 2,000 in attendance when I went to work with Buddy Harrison and my oldest son became the day-to-day pastor.

Let me tell you a little bit more about my church. As I said earlier, I did a lot of traveling for 14 years with FCF. In 2007, by the time Buddy Harrison died, I had mentored many people at the East Side Faith Community in Tucson, and I knew that God was speaking to me about taking the church. When that young pastor died, I knew God was asking me to pastor it and lead it through the grief and the loss of their pastor.

Our FCCI biannual conferences are like class or family reunions. When we meet, I have a chance to see many of the friends I made when I traveled to visit and speak at their churches. The main things I can give when our people come here for our conference are my attention and love, and impart to them revelation or anything God has given me.

Some of these ministers are phenomenal pastors in their native churches and they enrich all of us when they share their experiences and gifts at the FCCI conferences. We hold sessions throughout the week when we hear from the elders. I speak, Carl speaks, Reggies speaks. We welcome everybody. We feed and house them while they're here. It's a time of great fellowship and it builds up the international attendees who come and are reassured they are not out there by themselves.

As you are aware, Dr. Reggies has agreed to become the general superintendent of FCCI. I don't think Carl could have chosen anyone better prepared and equipped to follow in his footsteps. I think Dr. Regg is phenomenal. He is intelligent and wonderful and anointed. He has a great call on his life. He has come through many trials and he's been victorious. I have the utmost confidence in his leadership capabilities.

When someone considers joining FCCI, I tell them that I don't know any denomination or network of churches with an arm of missions that is more active or productive than FCCI. As I write, COVID-19 has impacted the world and our partners where they live and minister. Some of our pastors and elders have fallen ill with the virus. We have paid hospital and doctor bills where we could. We've sent computers. We are a funding arm for a lot of these international churches, in addition to being a source of relationship and advice.

There's always room for more partners in FCCI—always. I would like for us to grow more in the U.S. Keep in mind we are not an arm of a denomination but rather a mix of independent churches. I hope in some way we can appeal to independent churches that would like to get involved in missions to look at us, see our structure, and then join us in the wonderful work being done.

★★★★★

*Ebenezer Omobude*
*Pastor of Refinery New Covenant Gospel Church*
*Benin City, Nigeria*

As I write, COVID-19 has created a year with ministry scenarios that have been different and unexpected for everyone. At one point, everything we did had to be shut down. It was tough. Over the course of that year, God helped me grow right along with the church. My church was able to reach out to a lot of new people. We were able to pull resources together to help families stay on their feet. Economically, things are getting more expensive. The rate of inflation is pretty high, but God is helping us pull through.

My church is the Refinery New Covenant Gospel Church, a branch of the main church. We founded it on April. 28, 2019. It's a church that attracts a younger generation. We are still holding to the same tenets of the main church, still preaching the gospel of Christ, but reaching younger people. We are helping them understand what it means to be in this world, in this current system, and still love and fear God, while having a heart for the things of God.

My father, Felix Omobude, was one of the original founders and members of FCCI. He founded our mother church, New Covenant Gospel Church, and started our network of churches, Gospel Light International Ministries. We also have the outreach arm that is named LifeLink International which caters to the needs of the needy, homeless, and those who are in the hospital. We also have a few schools: Covenant Christian Academy, Lighthouse Polytechnic, and GLIM Bible College.

Since 2013, my father has led the Pentecostal churches in Nigeria. He just recently handed that duty over to another leader and it's good to have him back home. He started the church in 1988 and it has been an awesome experience. The one thing that stands out is the integrity he has maintained over the years. I'm grateful we have a strong foundation to build on. If there's anything my dad has done for the ministry and for us, not just speaking as his son but also as a pastor in the church, is that he has laid a good foundation, spiritually and morally. We have all been able to build on that.

I have grown up around FCCI over the years and I've come to appreciate the heart of love they have for those of us in the fields of our nations. It is a special thing to be in a developed country, reaching out to pastors in developing nations. FCCI establishes and build on relationship and fellowship. When they would hold conferences in our church and Dr. Carl Conley would come in, we forged a special bond and relationship with him and those who came with him.

I've been privileged to attend the FCCI conferences in the U.S. and Malawi, and it has taught me about being part of the family of God, that there are no natural, racial, or ethnic boundaries between us. Everybody comes together under the umbrella of fellowship so we can grow and learn from one another.

We're blessed now to have Dr. Reggies as our leader. It gives us, the younger generation, something to look forward to, something that we, in a few years to come, will be proud of because we made our mark and helped build it. I feel it's time for FCCI to have a wider, more global reach. We are going to give it our all to make FCCI known. We want to reach out to different nations of the world. By the grace of God, we have amazing leadership. It's time.

My wife and I were privileged to study at Southwestern Christian University in Bethany, Oklahoma under the leadership of and through the influence of Dr. Reggies. That also gave us a bigger picture of what God is doing in the world. It exposed our minds to many important concepts in our educational pursuit that have contributed to our ministry growth and success. In my ministry, it has helped me have a global perspective. I can speak anywhere and to a large audience because of what I have seen and learned from FCCI and its leaders—and from my degree training.

My wife finished her master's degree through Southwestern University and also had an awesome experience. Since 2019, she has been doing amazing work in the church. She has a women's ministry called Made of Honor Outreach through which she's able to reach out to younger and middle-aged ladies. I try to keep up with her but she is dynamic.

Through the years, I observed firsthand the impact FCCI had on my father and our ministry. I heard him say how much FCCI and being a part of it meant to him. I saw FCCI's heart of service and compassion. I was privileged one year to attend an FCCI conference in Arizona where I met people from India, from different nations in Africa like Malawi and South Africa, and even my own nation of Nigeria. It got into my heart at the conference that we are called to live a life of love that is real and relevant. In church, many times we pretend and feign obedience and joy, but in FCCI, I have seen that the love of God is real and practical.

I should also mention my mother who is wonderful and has been a source of strength and support for my father as he traveled and ministered so widely while she was back home. I know it has been her prayers that have held me and kept me in God's grace—and held our family together. She has helped my dad over the years hold down the fort. As with any leader, my dad had certain aspects of ministry he would not pay much attention to, so she would make sure those things were done. She would help put the people in order with her impressive administrative gift.

Mom and Dad founded Gospel Light Ministries in the backyard of our home. Both my parents have placed a strong emphasis on outreach and discipleship. Dad never emphasized preaching about prosperity but when it came to holiness or salvation, he knew those two issues were important and he structured a church and ministry to ensure they were paramount. Over the years, Dad has conducted many crusades and Dr. Carl has ministered in a lot of those as well as in our conferences to help us reach people with the gospel of Christ.

I would say to my family and friends in FCCI to get ready because we're about to be one of the biggest things God is doing on the face of the earth. I'm glad to be part of the family and to be able to see it.

★★★★★

Priscilla Mgala<br>Lead Apostle of Agape Life Church International – Malawi

Now that my husband who was the apostolic oversight for our churches has passed away into God's presence, I have assumed the role of the apostleship and presidency of Agape Life Church. The transition has been smooth. The pastors and staff have helped me get through it, so by God's grace I am happy to report that we are doing well. Of course, this transition has occurred during the COVID-19 pandemic, which did not hit us especially hard in 2020 but has in 2021. Since January of 2021, many people have passed on and many others have suffered. There has been some recovery but so many have died across the country. Ministers of the Lord and ministers of the government, along with everybody else have been affected. We have lost a lot of people.

We have tried to maintain a church presence during the pandemic so people could connect with us in person and online. The government limited our meetings to 50 people after having the limit set at 100 with a social distancing requirement of people being two meters apart. Our church meets twice on Sunday morning for 90 minutes. Then we bring in some other people. That is where I minister. In other branches of Agape Life Church, they do the same.

We have more than 70 churches and congregations in Malawi that include about 100 ministers of the gospel. We have coordinated effectively during the pandemic through Zoom and WhatsApp to connect with our people wherever they are. We also have more than 70 churches in Mozambique and the two in South Africa. They are all intact and doing well.

In 1992, Augustine, my husband, met with Dr. Carl Conley in Botswana. When they met, their hearts were joined together, and later Dr. Carl ordained him as a minister. At that time, they were part of FCF. When Dr. Carl left to start FCCI, we had to join him because we felt we were connected to him more than to the FCF. My husband was made the overseer and coordinator for Africa, and served in that role until his departure. We have been connected from the time Dr. Carl started FCCI.

We were part of FCF and now FCCI because we felt it important to be in something bigger and more comprehensive than we are. FCCI is an organization with which we share a common vision. It's also an organization where we have always felt welcome. We could feel the brotherly love. We were like sons and daughters and the teachings have equipped us for effective ministry. We felt that this is the group we needed to join because it has always helped us run with the vision God had given us. It has already been mentioned that in 2017, we held the FCCI biannual conference in Malawi.

It was wonderful to have the event in my country. It

continues to have an impact on the pastors and ministers of different churches throughout the nation. Many people joined FCCI from other congregations not only in Malawi, but also from throughout southern Africa. The different ministers who came to Malawi from all over the world really made an impact. Leaders are still talking about it.

Because of that, even after the departure of my husband, all the ministers were joined together. They were praying for us as a family. Even now, we have seen so much brotherly love and we are grateful. The conference brought us together as one entity. The church is strong in Malawi. The ministers have come together and are working together.

When my husband went home to be with the Lord in 2020, FCCI really supported us. When I told Dr. Reggies that Augustine was in the hospital, he was there for me. He would pray over and with me. Dr. Carl was there for us as well as was Bishop Silindza and Bishop Mapfumo. After Augustine died, I was strengthened by all who prayed for me, for my family, and for my children who are in the U.S. They managed to help us through the money they sent for the funeral services. We felt we were covered by FCCI.

Several years ago and after the conference in Malawi, my husband and I attended the FCCI conference in South Africa. That really brought us together and helped us make friends with new people. The teachings there were phenomenal and so uplifting and edifying. We knew the pastors and men of God who were ministering to us were there for us, and that really helped us grow deep in our spirit and faith. We brought our pastors from Malawi and it was a good investment to do so. They are still talking about what they learned and the impact it had. We also prepared and commended four leaders who were presented at the conference and ordained through FCCI. One of them is my sister who is the current ambassador from Malawi to the nation of Zimbabwe.

As I write, I plan to attend the conference in 2021 in Tucson, Lord willing. I hope the travel restrictions are not such that I will not be able to travel. Since my husband's passing, I have been carrying a lot of responsibility and I look forward to a time of refreshing there. I will also visit my family while I am there.

I have three daughters in the United States. One is living in Texas and two are in Oklahoma. I also have my son there who recently immigrated to Canada. My firstborn son, Augustine Jr., is still here. All my children have been impacted by FCCI. They're all telling me that they will come to the conference so they too can get refreshed. All my children attended universities in the U.S. where Dr. Wenyika helped them apply and gain admission. We consider Dr. Reggies to be their second father because he looked after them so well—and is still looking after them.

Let me close by emphasizing that FCCI is an organization that cares for and loves God's people and servants. They stand by the truth of loving God and people. I have seen and experienced it. To me, it is not just another organization, it is a family that cares for His people. They really encourage us as brothers and sisters to love one another and God. Those who are interested in FCCI, I call upon you to come and join this organization and I promise you'll never be the same. You will be impacted spiritually and be strengthened to go forward and accomplish the vision God has given you.

★★★★★

*Pastor Fred Alvarenga*
*Templo Cristiano Palabra de Fe*
*Dallas, Texas*

I joined Faith Community Church International after having been a pastor in Texas for many years and have been with that ministry ever since. I had been part of Faith Christian Fellowship (FCF) but made the transition because I knew Dr. Carl. Since I had not received much communication from FCF over the years and after Buddy Harrison died, things were not the same. I really believe all leaders should belong to a church network or organization and get involved. I have been out with Dr. Carl Conley on two or three occasions, and it has been quite helpful to me.

Even though I am pastor of a local church, I enjoy having the chance to go out and evangelize. Also, FCCI has held one conference in my church and I hope they will have more. I also went to Malawi and South Africa for their biannual conferences, and it was quite a blessing to be there. It was impressive in South Africa to see Dr. Conley turn the leadership over to Dr. Wenyika. Many leaders don't do that until they have no choice, but Dr. Carl did it now and it was a blessing to all of us.

FCCI gave me my first opportunity to go to Africa after I had already traveled to Europe and South America. Here locally, I fellowship with many Hispanic pastors. We meet and pray together every Tuesday in different places. That is not an organization, it's just a group of pastors. I hope FCCI will eventually expand its ministry into the Hispanic world for those pastors I pray with need to be involved with something bigger than they are that connects them to the world.

I have greatly benefited from being part of FCCI. It gives me a chance to talk to other pastors and to seek guidance and direction concerning issues that arise in ministry. I would urge anyone looking for a place to connect that will inspire and equip you for ministry to consider FCCI. I look forward to meeting you at one of our conferences.

★★★★★

*George Kajanga*
*Church Administrator, Agape Life Church International – Malawi*

I'm the church administrator in Malawi for Agape Life Church, which means I'm the head of all administrative matters within the church network. I report directly to the president of the church, and along with the president we have a vice-president and then the administrator. After that, there are other directors. I deal with the day-to-day business of the pastors, which involves communicating information from the president to them. I also process reports, something that is important so we have the data to understand what is happening and have the bigger picture.

We have a form we require each leader to fill out every Sunday that tells us how many people attended the church, if anyone was born again, the number of visitors, the offering, and other relevant information. If there was a miracle or noteworthy testimony, it is recorded in the report. Then we compile and distribute the data every month. It's important because once we have the data, it's easy to know what's going on—or isn't going on. Within my position, my responsibility is to make sure that I organize meetings, the board meeting, conferences, or at least structure a conference that's about to happen. I choose somebody who can head it up or set up a team that can run the event.

Our former leader, Brother Augustine, explained that FCCI is a matter of belonging to something with faith leaders from other nations. It is exciting to learn from one another. Many have said being part of FCCI has really broadened them because they have heard from so many outside Malawi, which is good. It connects them to the world and best practices of what's going on outside their borders. We have learned to value that affiliation so much.

I have had the chance to watch and learn how others approach their conferences and how they organize them, which is a little different from the way we do it. I have found it is a weakness with us in Africa that we organize a conference but when we get to the conference, we don't have the money for it. Then during the conference, we have to try and raise the money to feed people the next day or for the day after.

Also, I have noticed the amount of preparation that FCCI devotes to planning and logistics. That has challenged us to step up our game and be better at what we do. Plus, for the first time we have a chance to interact with South Americans and others from very far away. We get to see how much they love the Lord, and it makes us also want to love the Lord more because we see somebody from somewhere else giving their all for Him.

When the FCCI conference came to Malawi a few years ago, it was an unforgettable experience. It was the biggest thing any of us had been involved with locally. We had the largest number of visitors from other countries coming to our church we had ever had, and they had one goal: to learn and grow. The conference itself was well organized. It has left a mark on everybody. When we mention FCCI, everybody remembers something different that impressed them. Some remember the organization. Others remember the impact. Others just simply remember certain individuals they met or learned from.

When the conference came to Malawi, I connected with Dr. Reggies and served as the local organizer. I knew Dr. Regg was from Africa, but when he came in, it was not like a typical African. His style was totally different in getting things done. He's one person who has really impacted me with his ministry and administrative style.

I also had a chance to moderate the general sessions both here and in South Africa, and that was exciting. When I stood in front of people from other nations I was a bit intimidated and didn't want to make a mistake. At the same time, I was excited because I had the privilege of doing it. I learned many lessons that I then applied in South Africa when I was also asked to moderate the conference.

Many came from Malawi to South Africa because of how the conference in Malawi impacted them. That second time I knew more of what to expect and what was expected from me, and it flowed. Plus, we learned so much from the anointed speakers. Also, the ordination service was powerful to see so many coming forth to offer themselves to serve the Lord.

All things being equal, FCCI is a network that has the potential to grow and go into many nations because its message is a little different from what other groups have to offer. Some groups ask what others can put into it, but FCCI has a servant's heart and asks what they can give. They want everyone to take something home that will make them more effective.

FCCI may not look attractive and doesn't make statements about their own importance, but they reach out with love and that comes through loud and clear to people like me. I hope we recruit more aggressively and reach out to more while still being selective. I think we can help a lot of leaders and people of God. I hope we have more regional meetings also and not just rely on the biannual conference.

Pastor George Kajanga served as emcee at the conferences in both Malawi and South Africa

# CHAPTER SIX

# What FCCI Stands For

*I (Reggies) addressed who FCCI is and what we stand for in an earlier chapter. However, I thought I would include it again to make sure I did not miss anything and to give you a place that succinctly outlines who we are as a fellowship of churches for your future reference. Let's get started.*

## 1. WHO WE ARE

- We are a global network of leaders united to advance the kingdom of God by the establishment, strengthening, and multiplying of local churches. Also, we address the personal and professional development of Christian leaders and the edification of their respective church or parachurch members and followers.

- We treasure the richness of our multiethnic and multilingual diversity in a multinational fellowship.

- We organize ourselves for the purpose of edifying, uplifting, and encouraging others to exercise their God-given talents and gifts while giving them an opportunity to share their personal treasure with others.

- We play a supportive role as a resource for leaders in churches who are facing unique challenges along with the need to learn and grow from others.

- We are a fellowship that expects those who choose to be ordained or licensed though us to conduct themselves in accordance with the standards laid out in the Bible for ministers and Christian leaders as the elders of the fellowship interpret the Bible.

## 2. WHO WE ARE NOT

- We are not an organized denomination that prescribes or insists on a particular ecclesiology or eschatology.
- We are also not an international organization of churches.
- Though we engage in philanthropy, we are not a philanthropic organization.
- Though the individual leaders engage in national and global missions, FCCI facilitates and encourages participation but is not a missions organization.
- Though many are ordained, and thousands carry FCCI ministerial credentials worldwide, we are not an organization that requires ordination to belong. We do not require anyone to leave their current denominational affiliation as long as it meets their needs and their standards are compatible with the FCCI standard of believing in Jesus Christ as personal Lord and Savior and living a Spirit-empowered, Bible-honoring lifestyle.

## 3. WHAT WE DO

- We are intentional about having fellowship as brothers and sisters who are equal before the Lord, regardless of one's station in life or the importance of the position they hold in their lives, ministries, or churches.
- We gather regionally, nationally, and globally to rekindle our love for each other as brothers and sisters, to establish networks, and to familiarize one another with the work other brother and sisters are doing. Through these gatherings, we seek to encourage, equip, and enlighten leaders for leadership—in and out of the Church.
- Each network member is expected to explore ways through which they can minister and encourage other members.

- We encourage each network leader to cultivate a sensitivity for the needs of others in the fellowship and support them as the Lord leads.

## 4. WHAT WE DO NOT DO

- We do not own or will we ever lay claim to the property or assets owned by the individual ministries, organizations, or churches represented by the different leaders who are part of our global network and fellowship.

- We do not impose leadership over churches and organizations except by invitation or member initiated "apostolic" submission or recognition.

- FCCI is supported by its network members and does not have requirements that individuals, churches, or organizations give a portion of their income—although many have seen and enjoyed the blessing of doing so.

## 5. THE SEVEN PRINCIPLES OF THE FCCI STANDARD

a) Loving Dispositions

b) Intentional Inclusion

c) Faith-Driven Generosity

d) Biblical Equality and Esteem for All

e) Organic Fellowship and Interactions

f) Spirit-Empowered Living

g) Grace-Fortified Conduct

**a. Loving Dispositions** – A disposition is defined as a nature, characteristic, or personal trait of how we instinctively interact or comport ourselves with others. We expect all those who choose to be part of our fellowship to have a loving disposition towards others, irrespective of who they are, where they come from, or the titles they hold in life. Love is a non-negotiable Christian imperative and the greatest of all commandments: "A new commandment I give to you, that you love one another, even as I have loved you, that you also love one another. By this all men will know that you are My disciples, if you have love for one another" (John 13:34-35). Love distinguishes us from non-believers, not our talents, gifts, or church attendance numbers. All those things are important, however, for Paul wrote, "... faith, hope, love, abide these three; but the greatest of these is love" (1 Corinthians 13:13). True disciples of our Lord Jesus Christ maintain a loving disposition toward others:

> Beloved, let us love one another, for love is from God; and everyone who loves is born of God and knows God. The one who does not love does not know God, for God is love. By this the love of God was manifested in us, that God has sent His only begotten Son into the world so that we might live through Him. In this is love, not that we loved God, but that He loved us and sent His Son to be the propitiation for our sins. Beloved, if God so loved us, we also ought to love one another (1 John 4:7-11).

**b. Intentional Inclusion** – Through the person of Christ, we have all been included in one universal fellowship of believers.

> Therefore remember that previously you, the Gentiles in the flesh, who are called "Uncircumcision" by the so-called "Circumcision" which is performed in the flesh by human hands—remember that you were at that time separate from Christ, excluded from the people of Israel, and strangers to the covenants of the promise, having no hope and without God in the world. But now in Christ Jesus you who previously were far away have been brought near by the blood of Christ (Ephesians 2:11-13).

This is the template for intentional inclusion. God chose the undeserving to become the deserving, the foreigners to become citizens, sinners to become saints, and the distant to become near. All distinctions based on race, gender, citizenship, or religious hierarchy or affiliation were erased to create one new nation of believers united by their response to God's love through the person of Jesus Christ. We therefore expect every member of our fellowship to intentionally include other members in their circle of love.

Each one of us when left to our own devices will devolve to our baser or carnal instincts and behaviors that perpetuate differences, resulting in others feeling like they do not belong for reasons that have nothing to do with the values and standards of FCCI. We embrace and welcome into fellowship all brothers and sisters who identify with the faith tenets of FCCI, who choose to submit themselves to its leadership, and who agree to live by its stated standards. FCCI is a place for belonging and for many, a place called home.

**c. Faith-Driven Generosity** – Faith-driven generosity is giving ourselves to others and to the fellowship. It is defined as giving of our "time, treasure, and talent" to further the corporate purposes of the fellowship through intentionally blessing or assisting other members of the fellowship.

Generosity is a spirit, mindset, or disposition and has corresponding behaviors and actions: "For just as a human body without the spirit is a dead corpse, so faith without the expression of good works is dead!" (James 2:26, TPT). Generosity is an expression of good works. We expect every member to grow in their faith and trust in God demonstrated by a generous and selfless spirit toward others:

> Generosity brings prosperity but withholding from charity brings poverty. Those who live to bless others will have blessings heaped upon them, and the one who pours out his life to pour out blessings will be saturated with favor (Proverbs 11:24-25, TPT).

The Apostle Paul penned the well-known phrase, "It is more blessed to give than to receive." A reading of the entire segment of Scripture where that quote is contained reveals how Paul approached the whole subject of generosity:

> "So now, brethren, I commend you to God and to the word of His grace, which is able to build you up and give you an inheritance among all those who are sanctified. I have coveted no one's silver or gold or apparel.

71

Yes, you yourselves know that these hands have provided for my necessities, and for those who were with
me. I have shown you in every way, by laboring like
this, that you must support the weak. And remember
the words of the Lord Jesus, that He said, 'It is more
blessed to give than to receive'" (Acts 20:32-35).

Paul grew in faith and grace and consequently worked
hard to meet his own needs and those of his team while giving
freely to the churches he served. He used his talents and abilities to
create income and wealth to bless others who were in need. He did
not use his faith to amass wealth for himself. He distinguished his
apostolic ministry by his ability to meet his own needs *and* those of
others. In simple and clear terms, Paul was a giver and not a taker.
We desire the same for all who are part of the FCCI fellowship:

**d. Biblical Equality and Esteem for All** – Upholding
the "priesthood of all believers" as an unconditional or unquali-
fied biblical principle and value is a necessary practice in building or propagating a community or fellowship that fosters biblical
equality and esteem for all. Whether male or female, there is no
separate priesthood:

> But you are a chosen race, a royal priesthood, a holy
> nation, a people for God's own possession, so that you
> may proclaim the excellencies of Him who has called
> you out of darkness into His marvelous light; for you
> once were not a people, but now you are the people
> of God; you had not received mercy, but now you
> have received mercy (1 Peter 2:9-10).

We are all the same before the eyes of the Lord because
it is not what is outside but rather what is inside of us that matters, and we categorically reject partiality and ungodly preferential
treatment. We will give honor where and when it is due, but all
will be treated the same regardless of socioeconomic status, ec-
clesiastical title, or worldly achievements. The author James was
clear about this when he wrote to the first-century church in the
Diaspora,

> If, however, you are fulfilling the royal law according

to the Scripture, "You shall love your neighbor as yourself," you are doing well. But if you show partiality, you are committing sin and are convicted by the law as transgressors (James 2:8-9).

And then Paul added,

Therefore from now on we recognize no one according to the flesh; even though we have known Christ according to the flesh, yet now we know Him in this way no longer. Therefore if anyone is in Christ, he is a new creature; the old things passed away; behold, new things have come (2 Corinthians 5:16-17).

We are a fellowship that seeks not to recognize each other according to the flesh but rather in a manner described by God to the prophet Samuel:

"Do not look at his appearance or at the height of his stature, because I have rejected him; for God sees not as man sees, for man looks at the outward appearance, but the Lord looks at the heart" (1 Samuel 16:7).

Our concern is for what it is inside each of us and consequently our view of each other must be through the lens of love, humility, and mutual esteem one for another.

**e. Organic Fellowship and Interactions** – We encourage friendships and networking that is based on love for the brothers and sisters that fosters mutually beneficial interactions. Getting to know one another brings us closer to those who are like-minded and share the same interests. Our members should be those who are genuinely seeking to live "life with others" and are not looking for something to gain from connecting with others. We reject and lovingly expose those who enter the fellowship for the sole purpose of looking for opportunities to extract money or worldly goods from others:

Therefore, if there is any encouragement in Christ, if there is any consolation of love, if there is any fellowship of the Spirit, if any affection and compassion, make my joy complete by being of the same mind, maintaining the same love, united in spirit, intent on one purpose. Do nothing from selfishness or empty conceit, but with humility of mind regard one another as more important than yourselves; do not merely look out for your own personal interests, but also for the interests of others (Philippians 2:1-4).

**f. Spirit-Empowered Living** – We encourage all to cultivate their dependence on the Holy Spirit. Life should be approached holistically, and believers must allow the Holy Spirit to influence every facet of their being. Christian living requires us to respond to God holistically: "Hear, O Israel: The LORD our God, the LORD is one! You shall love the LORD your God with all your heart, with all your soul, and with all your strength" Deuteronomy 6:4-5, NKJV). This includes our entire being (spirit, soul, and body); our living (thinking/believing, affections or feelings); and our conduct, behaviors, and actions (orthodoxy, orthopathy, and orthopraxy).

Spirit-empowered *orthodoxy* is right thinking and right believing aided or directed by the Holy Spirit. Through this, we encounter and comprehend the truth for us to believe rightly. Spirit-empowered *orthopathy* is encouraging all to allow the Holy Spirit to influence and direct our emotions and feelings. Doing this allows us to overcome personal dispositions and feelings that inhibit our ability to love others unconditionally. The Holy Spirit enables us to apprehend what love is and what it is not.

Spirit-empowered *orthopraxy* results in right or correct actions and behaviors because of the personal influence, direction, and empowerment by the Holy Spirit. The Holy Spirit helps us align our conduct with God's expectations as revealed in the person of Jesus Christ and outlined in the Bible. Paul's prayer in Ephesians is instructive here:

> For this reason I bow my knees before the Father, from whom every family in heaven and on earth derives its name, that He would grant you, according to the riches of His glory, to be strengthened with power through His Spirit in the inner man, so that Christ

may dwell in your hearts through faith; and that you, being rooted and grounded in love, may be able to comprehend with all the saints what is the breadth and length and height and depth, and to know the love of Christ which surpasses knowledge, that you may be filled up to all the fullness of God (Ephesians 3:14-19).

**g. Grace-Fortified Conduct** – Our conduct as believers must be tempered by and fortified through the grace of God. An understanding of that grace (which is not the equivalent of permissiveness or tolerance) is a prerequisite for Bible-honoring believers. Additionally, the Bible is clear as to how we should conduct ourselves, thus biblical standards are achievable and expected. Believing in a biblical standard that is unchanging and clarified contextually by His Holy Spirit is an absolute necessity. God upholds the standard and gives every individual grace to reach that standard incrementally and progressively. Grace, therefore, enables us to have faith and live lives that please God and fulfill His good purposes or pleasure:

So then, my beloved, just as you have always obeyed, not as in my presence only, but now much more in my absence, work out your salvation with fear and trembling; for it is God who is at work in you, both to will and to work for His good pleasure (Philippians 2:12-13).

Simply put, grace is God's way of enabling initial and ongoing response to His love and subsequently manifests Bible-honoring conduct as we align our personal values with His.

★★★★★

*Also, here is some doctrinal information that can be found on our website and in our literature and documents.*

### Our Vision

Reach every nation with the contextualized holistic Gospel of Jesus Christ.

### Our Mission

Faith Community Churches International exists to facilitate and empower a multi-national, multi-faceted, multi-dimensional fellowship of ministers and churches who take the Great Commission seriously.

*Statement of Faith*

**We believe** in one God who is made up of three co-equal, co-eternal persons, namely, the Father, the Son, and the Holy Spirit.

**We believe** that God created man in His own image and has called him to manifest and reflect holiness through obedience to His commandments. Because man has failed in this responsibility and refused to honor God as God, man has fallen into a state of moral corruption, and has become alienated from his Creator.

But God, being rich in mercy, because of His great love, has initiated a plan of redemption and reconciliation for mankind, the pinnacle of which is found in the life, death, and resurrection of Jesus of Nazareth, the incarnation of God. He was conceived by the Holy Spirit, and born of the Virgin Mary, being at the same time fully God and fully man. He lived a sinless life, was crucified, died, and was buried. On the third day after His death, He rose again, and ascended into heaven, and now sits at the right hand of God the Father Almighty, and He will come again to judge the living and the dead.

Jesus Christ, through His substitutionary, atoning death and bodily resurrection, has provided the basis of our justification, which, by God's grace we receive by faith alone. God initiates this reconciliation through the regeneration of our hearts, which is witnessed by our repentance and confession of faith in the Lord Jesus Christ. Our great hope is the redemption of our bodies through resurrection to eternal life, which will complete our adoptions as sons and daughters.

As the supernatural and sovereign Agent in regeneration, the Holy Spirit places all believers into the body of Christ at the moment of salvation. He dwells in the hearts of every believer, effecting their regeneration, operating in their sanctification, instructing them into all truth, and sealing them until the day of redemption. In addition to this, the supernatural gifts of the Holy

Spirit are for the Church today, including the gift of speaking in other tongues.

**We believe** that the Bible, in its entirety, is divine revelation, and we submit to the authority of Holy Scripture, acknowledging it to be inerrantly inspired by God and carrying the full weight of His authority. Therefore, it alone is the standard for faith and practice.

## FCCI DISTINCTIVE

Our fellowship provides a godly accountability structure while demonstrating mutual respect and tolerance for different biblical views and ministry approaches. We do not compromise the full-gospel fundamentals of faith, and neither do we demand conformity to a particular viewpoint, music, or worship style. Faith Community Churches International is a Bible-centered community of faith. Our fellowship offers servant leadership to help and encourage our members in every possible way. Our leadership is open, available, and accountable. We believe today's successful churches must be more than preaching stations or "bless me clubs" where folks go to get a weekly religious "fix." The Church must get out of its self-focused circle and reach out to the world in a meaningful way. Our goal is to reach our nation and the world with a Bible-centered, culturally relevant, holistic Gospel. This involves every area of human life: food, clothing, housing, health care, education, economic development, and spiritual growth.

★★★★★

*There you have a bit more of who we are, what we believe, and what we expect. In the next chapter, I have included the names and a short bio sketch on each one of elders, some who have been mentioned or interviewed already. This should give you a good overview of the diversity that is part of FCCI.*

# CHAPTER SEVEN

# The FCCI Leaders and Elders

*Dr. Reggies Wenyika, General Superintendent*

Dr. Reggies Wenyika is general superintendent of FCCI. He was born in Harare, Zimbabwe. He served for ten years as Provost then President of Southwestern Christian University in Bethany Oklahoma, and currently serves as president of Ottawa University in Ottawa, Kansas.

A graduate of the University of Zimbabwe's College of Health and Sciences, Reggies also received a Bachelor of Religious Arts in Biblical Studies; a Master of Ministry in Leadership; a Master of Arts in Higher Education Administration; and a Doctor of Education in Higher Education Administration from Oral Roberts University where he was honored with the Most Outstanding Achievement Award. His wife of 24 years, Bongi, received her Ph.D. from the University of Oklahoma. They live in Ottawa, Kansas, and have two children, Thembi and Kudzai.

Dr. Reggies is a dynamic preacher and teacher regular sought as a speaker for conferences and large gatherings. He has a passion for education and helping youth find their place in life to live successfully and fruitfully. He brings great gifts to the leadership of FCCI and enriches all who know him.

*Dr. Carl E. Conley, Executive Vice President*

Dr. Carl E. Conley was raised among Native Americans

in Arizona U.S. as the son of missionary parents. For more than 30 years, he has served as a director of international humanitarian, community development, and church ministries, having traveled and ministered in 86 nations. He is a specialist at field development and management. He has earned bachelor's and master's degrees in theology, a doctorate in law, and a doctorate in international law. He currently serves as executive vice president of Faith Community Churches International with churches in 50 nations.

### Dr. Louise Brock, Elder

Dr. Louise Brock is a third-generation minister of the gospel. She is a noted scholar, author, and a Bible college curriculum creator, and is widely traveled and has been a sought-after speaker internationally for many years. She has led more than twenty Scholars Tours of Israel. She has served as a leader and director of domestic and international ministries for more than 25 years. She is a founding elder of Faith Community Churches International. She presently serves as Pastor of Faith Community Church East in Tucson, Arizona USA.

### Felix Omobude, Elder

Rev. Dr. Felix Ilaweagbon Omobude is the general superintendent of Gospel Light International Ministries (New Covenant Gospel Church), which he founded in 1988 with its international headquarters in Benin City, Nigeria. The church has branches spread across the nation as well as outside Nigeria. He has served two terms as the president of the Nigerian Pentecostal Fellowship, an organization with more than 18 million followers in Nigeria and the world over. In addition to his church duties, Dr. Felix has founded Covenant Christian Academy, Lighthouse Polytechnic, and GLIM Bible College.

### Solomon Mwesige, Elder

Solomon Mwesige is the senior pastor of Good News Church in Kampala, Uganda, one of the fastest-growing churches in the nation with more than 8,000 in attendance. It has branches all over the nation. He is the founder of King Solomon's Junior School. He directs the daily feeding of more than 50,000 refugee children in three settlements. He also founded the first Christian television station in his nation. He is sought after for his wisdom and knowledge in many different expressions of ministry.

### David Tranter, Elder

Before entering ministry, David was a successful sheep farmer in Northern Victoria, Australia. David has attained many degrees, the highest being a master's degree of theology. David is also a trained counselor. He is a man of great experience in the practical side of life, bringing that wisdom as it applies to ministry among people. He is a man of passion for the things of God. A man of faith who teaches and believes in the supernatural power of God in the lives of believers. In other words, David is a man of faith.

### Kingsley Ohangbon, Elder

In 1999, Bishop Kingsley Ohangbon arrived in Madrid, Spain with nothing but the shirt on his back. By the grace of God and God's love in his heart, he began his work of spreading the Word of God. He now is the presiding bishop of a large network of churches.

### Dr. Anne Wood-Torre, Elder

Rev. Dr. Anne Wood, missionary in Asia since 1995, founded Life Solutions in Abundance (LSA) in the Philippines in 2008 and currently serves as its executive director. She resides in the Philippines where LSA now focuses on reaching unreached people groups in the region and beyond.

### Javan Ommani, Elder

Bishop Javan Ommani leads a large widespread ministry with over 200 churches, a hospital, a Bible college serving much of Kenya, East Africa. He served for several years in the national parliament and is a highly respected leader and Christian states-man throughout his nation.

### Bishop Levy Silindza, Elder

Bishop Silindza is a highly effective teacher and sought–after conference speaker who specializes in training people to be leaders. He pastors a large and effective church, ministers in many nations, and is responsible for FCCI across the African continent. Bishop Silindza has also been very successful in business; he advises business leaders on keys to success.

I hope you have enjoyed learning a bit more about us through this book and I encourage you to get in touch with Dr. Carl or me if you have any questions.

Our contact information is as follows:

Dr. Carl Conley – carl4032@gmail.com

Dr. Reggies Wenyika – fcciclergy@gmail.com

You can also watch for updates on our work and ministry at our website:

https://www.fcciweb.com/

Pictured here is the late Apostle Augustine Mgala with his son-in-law, James Houston, who was ordained at the South Africa conference

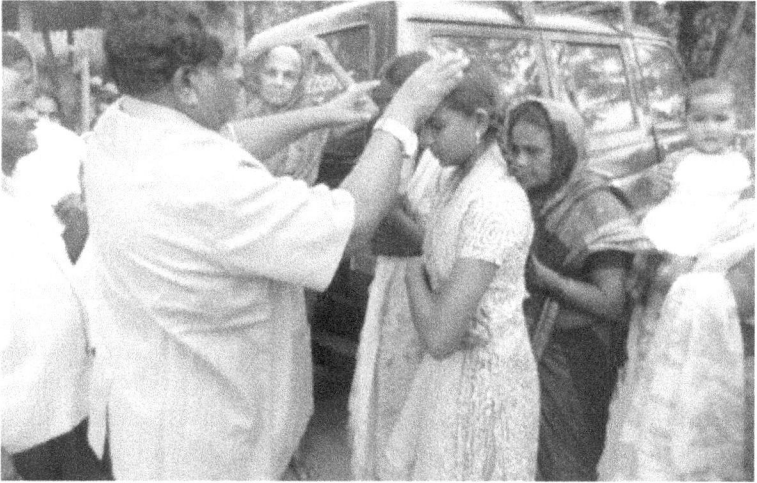

Bishop G. Thomas praying for people in India.

Dr. Reggies poses with the delegation from his native land of Zimbabwe at the South African conference.

**Dr. Carl Conley** has been active in the ministry for over five decades. In the last 30 years, he has served as a director of ministries that emphasized international humanitarian, community development, church growth and expansion, and has traveled and ministered in 86 nations. He founded FCCI and now serves as executive vice-president and chief operating officer. Carl holds a master's degree in theology, a Doctor of Jurisprudence in corporate law, and a Doctor of Jurisprudence in international law.

**Dr. Reggies Wenyika** has served as an educator, pastor, and missionary over the last 25 years and has traveled to many parts of the world as an ambassador for both Christ and education. Reggies also serves as a university president and took the reins of FCCI's leadership from Dr. Conley in 2019. He holds two master's degrees in education and in ministry, and a Doctor of Education degree.